Curry
BIBLE

Curry
BIBLE

EXOTIC AND FRAGRANT CURRIES

First published in 2010
LOVE FOOD is an imprint of Parragon Books Ltd

Parragon
Queen Street House
4 Queen Street
Bath BA1 1HE, UK

ISBN: 978-1-4075-9731-7

Additional recipes by Beverly LeBlanc, Judy Williams and Corinne Trang
New recipes by Linda Doeser
Edited by Fiona Biggs
Photography by Mike Cooper
Home economy by Sumi Glass, Carole Handslip and Lincoln Jefferson

Printed in China

Notes for the Reader

This book uses both metric and imperial measurements. Follow the same units of measurement throughout; do not mix metric and imperial. All spoon measurements are level: teaspoons are assumed to be 5 ml, and tablespoons are assumed to be 15 ml. Unless otherwise stated, milk is assumed to be full fat, eggs and individual vegetables are medium, and pepper is freshly ground black pepper.

The times given are an approximate guide only. Preparation times differ according to the techniques used by different people and the cooking times may also vary from those given. Optional ingredients, variations or serving suggestions have not been included in the calculations.

Recipes using raw or very lightly cooked eggs, fish, meat or poultry should be avoided by infants, the elderly, pregnant women, convalescents and anyone suffering from an illness. Pregnant and breastfeeding women are advised to avoid eating peanuts and peanut products. Sufferers from nut allergies should be aware that some of the ready-made ingredients used in the recipes in this book may contain nuts. Always check the packaging before use.

Picture Acknowledgements

The publisher would like to thank the following for permission to reproduce copyright material on the following pages:
Corbis: front cover (Ground cayenne pepper and cayenne peppers © Garcia/photocuisine/Corbis)
Getty Images: jacket flaps/endpapers (Green chillies © Ion-Bogdan DUMITRESCU/Getty Images), 6–7, 8, 18–19, 60–61, 104–105, 146–147, 188–189

Contents

Introduction

Curry is a firm favourite in almost every corner of the globe. Variations of this delicious spicy cuisine can be traced back to the dawn of civilization, and the wonderful colours, textures and flavours produced by the spices used in the preparation of curry have ensured its enduring popularity throughout the world. Spices had been used extensively in the kitchens of the wealthy in England since the late Middle Ages, both to preserve food and to disguise the flavour of ingredients that were past their best. With the opening up of the spice routes in the seventeenth and eighteenth centuries spices became less expensive and more readily available and began to be incorporated in everyday cooking. Meanwhile, the use of spices as flavourings had become something of a fine art in India and South-East Asia, regions that were extensively colonized by Western powers.

The cuisines of India, Cambodia, Burma, Malaysia, Indonesia and Vietnam were adapted to the palates of the foreign occupiers and were subsequently brought 'home'. When the British Raj in India came to an end in 1947, returning army personnel and civil servants brought their favourite recipes with them and curry became firmly established in Britain, becoming so popular in subsequent decades that it was recently voted the top British national dish. But what exactly is a 'curry'? There are almost as many explanations of the meaning of the word as there are different types of curry: however, the consensus is that it is a dish of meat, poultry, fish or vegetables cooked in one of many variants of spicy sauce, although the type of curry and the spices used varies from region to region and from country to country.

Cooking with Spices

Because spices are so widely available in India, curries from all over the subcontinent use a wider range of spices than any other region. Curries native to Malaysia, Thailand and Indonesia generally use fresh spices (ground into a paste) rather than dried spices. The curries of Northern India are thick, moderately spicy and creamy. Rice is not as popular as bread as an accompaniment here – this is the home of the naan. The hot humid climate of Southern India and an abundance of fresh fruit and vegetables have given rise to a cuisine largely based on vegetables, and seafood in the coastal areas. The hottest Indian curries come from here. There is a strong Malaysian and Chinese influence in the cuisine of Eastern India, which is based on rice, and vegetable dishes are popular. Western India has few vegetables, but peanuts and coconuts are widely grown and are routinely incorporated in the dishes from this region. There is great diversity here, with dishes ranging from the spicy curries of Rajasthan to the mild sweetness of Gujarati cuisine.

While India is synonymous with curry, other countries have also made a huge contribution – the more delicate Thai curries have become increasingly popular in the West in recent years. Those regions, such as Goa in Western India, and Cambodia and Vietnam in South-East Asia, that were colonized by European nations with a developed cuisine of their own, incorporated some of the flavours and cooking techniques of Portugal and France respectively, so their curries are different from those of Southern India and Indonesia.

Asian curries today have gained global recognition. There are thousands of Indian restaurants in Britain, and other Asian restaurants are also very popular.

The taste for curry has now spread across Europe and Asian restaurants have started appearing in all major European cities. Supermarkets are well stocked with Asian ingredients and making an authentic curry at home is now easier than ever, a trend that has travelled to many parts of the United States, Canada and Australia.

Cooking a curry may seem a little daunting if you've never done it before, but curries are actually very easy to prepare and you can't fail to impress. The most important ingredients in any curry are the spices, which have always been valued for the flavours, colours and aromas that they add to the most basic ingredients. You can gradually build up a supply of the spices you need for your favourite dishes so that you will always have them to hand.

When buying spices, look out for stalks, leaves or dust in the packaging, which can be an indication of inferior quality. Don't buy in bulk, as spices have a limited shelf life, losing their flavour and aroma if kept

for too long. Dried ground spices will keep in a cool, dark place for up to six months, while whole spices can be used for up to a year after purchase. Heat and light will contribute to a faster deterioration of the spices. Although commercial spices are traditionally kept in clear glass jars, an Indian spice tin with several compartments is a better option. If you don't have a sufficiently cool cupboard, you can store your spices in a plastic container in the refrigerator.

The heat in Indian curries used to come from black pepper, but when chillies were introduced to the subcontinent in the fifteenth century they replaced pepper as the main heat source. You can control the spiciness of any curry that contains chillies by including or omitting the seeds. These contain most of the heat of the chilli and can easily be removed if you prefer a milder dish. Do be careful when

deseeding, though – wear gloves, if possible, and avoid any contact with your eyes or skin.

If a recipe specifies that the spices should be cooked out or dry-roasted in a frying pan before being added to the dish, don't be tempted to ignore this instruction – if you decide to bypass it and add spices that have not been cooked they will give a raw taste to the finished dish. Do make sure not to substitute dried spices where fresh spices are specified – the dried and fresh varieties of any spice will usually have very different flavours and this will have a big impact on the finished dish. This is particularly important in the case of fresh or dried ginger and fresh or dried chillies. Fresh ginger root has a sweet taste and aroma, whereas the dried root is fiery with a distinct bite. As a general rule larger fresh chillies will not be as hot as smaller ones, and dried chillies will be hotter than the fresh varieties.

Equipment and utensils

You won't need any special kitchen utensils or equipment to cook curries, although the following will be useful:

food processor or blender
large, heavy-based, non-stick frying pan with a lid
large heavy-based saucepan
cast-iron griddle pan
wok
set of sharp knives
slotted spoons
pestle and mortar

Reasonably priced spice grinders are now widely available, and are a labour-saving alternative to a pestle and mortar. You could also use a coffee grinder to grind your spices; however, if you subsequently grind coffee in it, the coffee will be contaminated by the odour of the spices.

Essential Curry Ingredients

Aniseed
Anise is native to India and looks rather like a celery seed. It is related to caraway and cumin, but the flavour is more akin to that of thyme. Anise aids the digestion.

Asafoetida
Obtained from the resinous gum of a tropical plant, asafoetida can be bought from Asian stores in block or powder form. It should be used sparingly.

Bay leaf
The bay leaves used in curries are different from those used in the West. Asian bay leaves come from the cassia tree, whereas the Western ones are obtained from sweet bay laurel. Western bay leaves are a popular substitute, as the Asian ones are rarely available in the West.

Cardamom
Cardamom has been used in Asian cooking since ancient times. Whole cardamom pods are used to flavour rice and different types of sauces. Ground cardamom, used in many desserts and drinks, can be bought from most Asian stores, but grinding small quantities at home will produce better flavours.

Chilli powder
Rich red ripe chillies are dried to obtain dried red chillies. Chilli powder is made by finely grinding dried red chillies. Crushed dried chillies are made by grinding dried red chillies to a coarse texture. These are sold in Asian stores.

Chillies, fresh
Chillies come in different sizes, strengths and colours. Generally, the small thin ones are hot while the large fleshy ones tend to be milder. Most of the heat is in the seeds and the membrane.

Cinnamon
One of the oldest spices, cinnamon is obtained from the dried bark of a tropical plant related to the laurel. It has a warm flavour and is used in both savoury and sweet dishes.

Cloves
Cloves are the unripened dried buds of a Southern Asian evergreen tree. They have a strong distinctive flavour and are used both whole and ground in Asian cuisine.

Coconut
Coconut milk is made by grating, blending and squeezing the juice from the flesh of coconuts. The first extraction is thicker and the second, which is made from the remaining blended coconut by soaking it in water, is thinner. The second extraction can be boiled for a longer time than the first, which releases too much of the oil when it is boiled. Canned coconut milk is an ideal substitute for the second extraction.

Creamed coconut comes in a block and is readily available in supermarkets. It can be used to replace the first extraction from a fresh coconut and should be added towards the end of cooking time.

Desiccated coconut is grated fresh coconut that has been dried to prolong its shelf life. It is used in both sweet and savoury dishes, including a variety of desserts and sweetmeats. Coconut milk can be made by soaking desiccated coconut in hot milk and blending it in an electric blender.

Coriander, fresh
The fresh leaves of the coriander plant are widely used in Asian cuisine for flavouring and garnishing. Coriander leaves also form the basis of many chutneys and pastes.

Coriander seeds

The fruit produced by the mature coriander plant is the seed that is used as a spice. The sweet, mellow flavour is very important in South-East Asian curries.

Cumin

Cumin is used either whole or ground. It has a warm and assertive taste. The whole seeds are used to flavour the oil for many vegetarian dishes and the ground version is used in curries. There are two varieties: black and white. Each has its own distinct flavour and one cannot be substituted for the other. Black cumin seeds are sometimes mistaken for caraway seeds.

Curry leaves

A hallmark of Southern Indian cooking, these have an assertive flavour. Fresh and dried versions are sold in Asian shops. Dried ones can be stored in an airtight jar and fresh ones can be frozen.

Curry powder and curry pastes

Curry powder is a British invention that was created in Southern India and exported to Britain when the British returned home at the end of the Raj. It is produced by blending several spices together, making it easier to create curries. In India, spices are individually blended during cooking and curry powder is never used. It is, however, a popular ingredient in South-East Asian curries.

Curry pastes are commonly used in South-East Asian cooking and are made in a similar way to curry powder, but oil is added to the powdered spices in order to make a paste. Doing this helps to preserve the wet spice blends, giving a superior flavour to curries. The tradition of curry pastes may have originated in the Indian and South-East Asian practice of adding water to spices when grinding them with a grinding stone.

Fennel seeds

These have a taste similar to that of anise. They have been used in curries since ancient times.

Fenugreek

A strong and aromatic herb, fenugreek is cultivated in India and Pakistan, but is native to the Mediterranean region. The fresh leaves are cooked like spinach in a variety of ways, and they are dried and used in smaller quantities to flavour meat and poultry dishes.

Fenugreek seeds are used to flavour vegetables, lentils and some fish dishes. They have a distinctive and powerful flavour, and should be used only in very small quantities.

Fish sauce

Fish sauce is one of the most common ingredients in South-East Asian cooking, especially that of Thailand, where it is known as nam pla. It is made from anchovies packed with salt; the liquid released by the fish is collected and sold as fish sauce.

Galangal

This comes in two varieties: greater galangal, also known as Laos ginger or Thai ginger, and lesser galangal. The former is more widely available and is an essential ingredient in most South-East Asian curries, especially those from Thailand. It has a creamy white flesh and a distinctive, pine-like aroma. Lesser galangal, with its orange-tinged flesh, has a stronger and hotter flavour.

Garam masala

The word garam means 'heat' and masala refers to the blending of different spices that are believed to create body heat. The basic ingredients in garam masala are cinnamon, cardamom, cloves and black pepper. Other spices are added to these, according to preference.

Garlic

Fresh garlic is an integral part of Asian cooking. Dried flakes, powder and garlic salt cannot create the same authentic flavour. Garlic is always used crushed, minced or puréed. It is beneficial in reducing the level of cholesterol in the blood and its antiseptic properties aid the digestive system.

To make garlic purée, peel at least 6 large bulbs of garlic and purée in a blender. To store in the refrigerator for immediate use, preserve the purée in cooking oil and store in an airtight jar for 3–4 weeks. Alternatively, divide into small portions, freeze and use as required. You can buy ready-made garlic purée, but the home-made version has a superior flavour.

Ghee

Ghee has a rich and distinctive flavour and is used liberally in Mogul food. There are two types of ghee: pure butterfat ghee and vegetable ghee. Butterfat ghee is made from unsalted butter and vegetable ghee from vegetable shortening. Ghee can be heated to a high temperature without burning. Both types are available from Indian stores and larger supermarkets. Unsalted butter can be used in some dishes, but cannot be heated to the same temperature.

Ginger

Like garlic, fresh ginger is a vital ingredient in curry making. It has a warm, woody aroma.

To make ginger purée, peel the ginger with a potato peeler, chop roughly and purée in a blender. To store in the refrigerator for immediate use, preserve the purée in cooking oil and store in an airtight jar. This will keep for 3–4 weeks. Alternatively, divide the purée into small portions, freeze and use as required. Ready-made ginger purée should be preserved in oil and not citric acid, which tends to impair the flavour.

Lemon grass

Lemon grass has an intensely lemony flavour without the acidity of the fruit. It is widely used in South-East Asian curries, soups, curry pastes and pickles. Dried and ground lemon grass, known as 'serai powder', makes a good alternative to fresh. Fresh lemon grass can be frozen successfully.

Limes/kaffir lime leaves

Kaffir limes are widely used throughout South-East Asia. They lend an intense lemony bouquet to curries and curry pastes.

Kaffir lime leaves can be used either whole or finely shredded – the latter method imparts a superior flavour. They can be frozen and used as required.

Mustard seeds

Mustard seeds are an essential ingredient in vegetarian cooking. Black and brown mustard seeds are the ones most commonly used, with the white ones being reserved for making pickles. Black and brown seeds lend a nutty flavour to the dish.

Nigella seeds

These tiny black seeds are also known as onion seeds because of their striking resemblance. The seeds are used whole for flavouring vegetables, pickles, breads and snacks.

Palm sugar

This dark, unrefined sugar is made from the sap of the coconut palm tree. It is also referred to as jaggery. It has a sweet wine-like flavour and usually comes in the form of a solid cake with a crumbly texture.

Peppercorns

Fresh green berries are dried in the sun to obtain black pepper. Green berries come from the pepper vine native to the monsoon forests of south-western India. Whole black peppercorns will keep well in an airtight jar, but ground black pepper loses its wonderful aromatic flavour very quickly – it is best to grind as needed.

Poppy seeds

The opium poppy, grown mainly in the tropics, produces the best poppy seeds. There are two varieties: white and black. The white seeds are ground and added to curries to give them a nutty flavour. They are also used as a thickener and as a topping for naan.

Rosewater/rose essence

Rosewater is the diluted essence of a special strain of edible rose, the petals of which are used to garnish Mogul dishes.

Rose essence is very concentrated and should be used sparingly as a substitute for rosewater.

Saffron

The saffron crocus grows extensively in Kashmir in Northern India. Around 250,000 stamens of this crocus are needed to produce just 450 g/1 lb of saffron. Although expensive, saffron is a highly concentrated ingredient and only minute quantities are required to flavour and colour any dish.

Sesame seeds

These pale seeds have a rich and nutty flavour. They may be sprinkled on naan before baking, ground to a paste for thickening sauces, and used with vegetables and some sweet dishes.

Shrimp paste

A popular ingredient in South-East Asian curries, shrimp paste is made from fermented shrimps or prawns, pounded with salt into a paste. It is also known as 'terasi', 'blachan' and 'balachan', and it has a strong, fishy and salty flavour.

Tamarind

Resembling pea pods at first, tamarind turns dark brown with a thin hard outer shell when ripe. The chocolate-brown flesh is encased in the shell with seeds, which have to be removed. The flesh is sold dried and has to be soaked in hot water to yield a pulp. Ready-to-use concentrated tamarind pulp or juice is quick and easy to use. Valued for its distinctive flavour, tamarind is added to vegetables, lentils, peas, chutneys and fish and seafood dishes.

Turmeric

Fresh turmeric rhizomes resemble fresh ginger, with a beige-brown skin and bright yellow flesh. Fresh turmeric is dried and ground to produce this essential spice, which should be used in small quantities.

Essential Recipes

Thai Green Curry Paste

- 1 tbsp coriander seeds
- 1 tbsp cumin seeds
- 12 fresh green bird's eye chillies, chopped
- 5 garlic cloves, chopped
- 2 lemon grass stalks, chopped
- 5 fresh kaffir lime leaves, chopped
- handful of fresh coriander, chopped
- finely grated rind of 1 lime
- 1 tsp salt
- 1 tsp black peppercorns, crushed

Heat a dry frying pan until hot, add the coriander and cumin seeds and cook over a medium–high heat, shaking the frying pan frequently, for 2–3 minutes, or until starting to pop. Put the toasted seeds in a food processor or small blender with all the remaining ingredients and process to a thick, smooth paste. Transfer to a screw-top glass jar and store in the refrigerator for up to a week.

Thai Red Curry Paste

- 1 tbsp coriander seeds
- 1 tbsp cumin seeds
- 12 dried red chillies, chopped
- 2 shallots, chopped
- 6 garlic cloves, chopped
- 2.5-cm/1-inch piece fresh ginger, chopped
- 2 lemon grass stalks, chopped
- 4 fresh kaffir lime leaves, chopped
- handful of fresh coriander, chopped
- finely grated rind of 1 lime
- 1 tsp salt
- 1 tsp black peppercorns, crushed

Heat a dry frying pan until hot, add the coriander and cumin seeds and cook over a medium–high heat, shaking the frying pan frequently, for 2–3 minutes, or until starting to pop. Put the toasted seeds in a food processor or small blender with all the remaining ingredients and process to a thick, smooth paste. Transfer to a screw-top glass jar and store in the refrigerator for up to a week.

Thai Yellow Curry Paste

- 3 small fresh orange or yellow chillies, chopped
- 3 garlic cloves, chopped
- 4 shallots, chopped
- 3 tsp ground turmeric
- 1 tsp salt
- 12–15 black peppercorns, crushed
- 1 lemon grass stalk (white part only), chopped
- 2.5-cm/1-inch piece fresh ginger, chopped

Put all the ingredients in a food processor or small blender and process to a thick, smooth paste. Transfer to a screw-top glass jar and store in the refrigerator for up to a week.

Masaman Curry Paste

- 4 large dried red chillies
- 2 tsp shrimp paste
- 3 shallots, finely chopped
- 3 garlic cloves, finely chopped
- 2.5-cm/1-inch piece fresh galangal, chopped
- 2 lemon grass stalks (white part only), finely chopped
- 2 cloves
- 1 tbsp coriander seeds
- 1 tbsp cumin seeds
- seeds from 3 green cardamom pods
- 1 tsp black peppercorns
- 1 tsp salt

Cut off and discard the chilli stalks and place the chillies in a bowl. Cover with hot water and soak for 30–45 minutes. Wrap the shrimp paste in foil and grill or dry-fry for 2–3 minutes, turning once or twice. Remove from the grill or frying pan. Dry-fry the shallots, garlic, galangal, lemon grass, cloves, coriander seeds, cumin seeds and cardamom seeds over a low heat, stirring frequently, for 3–4 minutes, until lightly browned. Transfer to a food processor and process until finely ground. Add the chillies and their soaking water and the peppercorns and salt, and process again. Add the shrimp paste and process again to a smooth paste. Transfer to a screw-top glass jar and store in the refrigerator for up to a week.

Penang Curry Paste

- 8 large dried red chillies
- 2 tsp shrimp paste
- 3 shallots, chopped
- 5-cm/2-inch piece fresh galangal, chopped
- 8 garlic cloves, chopped
- 4 tbsp chopped coriander root
- 3 lemon grass stalks (white part only), chopped
- grated rind of 1 lime
- 1 tbsp fish sauce
- 2 tbsp vegetable or groundnut oil
- 1 tsp salt
- 6 tbsp crunchy peanut butter

Cut off and discard the chilli stalks and place the chillies in a bowl. Cover with hot water and soak for 30–45 minutes. Wrap the shrimp paste in foil and grill or dry-fry for 2–3 minutes, turning once or twice. Put the chillies and their soaking water into a blender or food processor. Add the shrimp paste, shallots, galangal, garlic, coriander root and lemon grass and process until finely chopped. Add the lime rind, fish sauce, oil and salt and process again. Add the peanut butter and process to make a thick paste. Transfer to a screw-top glass jar and store in the refrigerator for up to a week.

Garlic & Ginger Paste

- 1–2 garlic bulbs, separated into cloves, roughly chopped
- large piece fresh ginger, roughly chopped

Put equal weights of garlic and ginger in a food processor or small blender and process to a smooth paste. Transfer to a screw-top glass jar and store in the refrigerator for up to a week.

Garam Masala

- 2 bay leaves, crumbled
- 2 cinnamon sticks, broken in half
- seeds from 8 green cardamom pods
- 2 tbsp cumin seeds
- 1½ tbsp coriander seeds
- 1½ tsp black peppercorns
- 1 tsp cloves
- ¼ tsp ground cloves

Heat a dry frying pan over a high heat until a splash of water 'dances' when it hits the surface. Reduce the heat to medium, add the bay leaves, cinnamon sticks, cardamom seeds, cumin seeds, coriander seeds, peppercorns and cloves and dry-fry, stirring constantly, until the cumin seeds look dark golden brown and you can smell the aromas. Immediately tip the spices out of the pan and leave to cool. Use a spice grinder or pestle and mortar to grind the spices to a fine powder. Stir in the ground cloves. Store in an airtight container for up to 2 months.

Ghee

- 250 g/9 oz butter

Melt the butter in a large heavy-based saucepan over a medium heat and continue simmering until a thick foam appears on the surface of the butter. Continue simmering, uncovered, for 15–20 minutes, or until the foam separates, the milk solids settle on the bottom and the liquid becomes clear and golden.

Meanwhile, line a sieve with a piece of muslin and place the sieve over a bowl. Slowly pour the liquid through the muslin, without disturbing the milk solids at the bottom of the pan. Discard the milk solids.

Leave the ghee to cool, then transfer to a smaller container, cover and chill. Store in the refrigerator for up to 4 weeks.

Paneer

- 2.2 litres/4 pints milk
- 6 tbsp lemon juice

Pour the milk into a large heavy-based saucepan over a high heat and bring to the boil. Remove the pan from the heat and stir in the lemon juice. Return the pan to the heat and continue boiling for a further minute, until the curds and whey separate and the liquid is clear. Remove the pan from the heat and set aside for an hour or so, until the milk is completely cool. Meanwhile, line a sieve with a piece of muslin large enough to hang over the edge and place the sieve over a bowl.

Pour the curds and whey into the muslin, then gather up the edges and squeeze out all the excess moisture.

Use a piece of string to tightly tie the muslin around the curds in a ball. Put the ball in a bowl and place a plate on top. Place a food can on the plate to weigh down the curds, then chill in the refrigerator for at least 12 hours. The curds will press into a compact mass that can be cut. The paneer will keep for up to 3 days in the refrigerator.

Chapter 1
Poultry

Pistachio Chicken Korma

Serves 4

ingredients

- 115 g/4 oz shelled pistachio nuts
- 200 ml/7 fl oz boiling water
- good pinch of saffron threads, pounded
- 2 tbsp hot milk
- 700 g/1 lb 9 oz skinless, boneless chicken breasts or thighs, cut into 2.5-cm/1-inch cubes
- 1 tsp salt, or to taste
- ½ tsp pepper
- juice of ½ lemon
- 55 g/2 oz ghee or unsalted butter
- 6 green cardamom pods
- 1 large onion, finely chopped
- 2 tsp garlic purée
- 2 tsp ginger purée
- 1 tbsp ground coriander
- ½ tsp chilli powder
- 280 g/10 oz natural yogurt, whisked
- 150 ml/5 fl oz single cream
- 2 tbsp rosewater
- 6–8 white rose petals, washed, to garnish
- cooked basmati rice and lemon wedges, to serve

1 Put the pistachio nuts into a heatproof bowl with the boiling water and soak for 20 minutes. Meanwhile, soak the saffron in the hot milk.

2 Put the chicken in a non-metallic bowl and add the salt, pepper and lemon juice. Rub the mixture into the chicken, then cover and leave to marinate in the refrigerator for 30 minutes.

3 Heat a medium-sized, heavy-based saucepan over a low heat, then add the ghee. Add the cardamom pods, and when they have puffed up, add the onion and increase the heat to medium. Cook, stirring frequently, for 8–9 minutes until the onion is a pale golden colour.

4 Add the garlic purée and ginger purée and cook, stirring frequently, for a further 2–3 minutes. Add the coriander and chilli powder and cook, stirring, for 30 seconds. Add the chicken, increase the heat to medium–high and cook, stirring constantly, for 5–6 minutes until the chicken changes colour.

5 Reduce the heat to low and add the yogurt and the saffron and milk mixture. Bring to a slow simmer, cover and cook for 15 minutes. Stir halfway through to ensure that it does not stick to the base of the pan.

6 Meanwhile, put the pistachio nuts and their soaking water in a blender or food processor and process until smooth. Add to the chicken mixture, followed by the cream. Cover and simmer, stirring occasionally, for a further 15–20 minutes. Stir in the rosewater and remove from the heat. Garnish with the rose petals and serve immediately with cooked basmati rice and lemon wedges.

Kashmiri Chicken

Serves 4–6

ingredients

- seeds from 8 green cardamom pods
- ½ tsp coriander seeds
- ½ tsp cumin seeds
- 1 cinnamon stick
- 8 black peppercorns
- 6 cloves
- 1 tbsp hot water
- ½ tsp saffron threads
- 40 g/1½ oz ghee or 3 tbsp vegetable oil or groundnut oil
- 1 large onion, finely chopped
- 2 tbsp Garlic and Ginger Paste (see page 15)
- 250 ml/9 fl oz natural yogurt
- 8 skinless, boneless chicken thighs, sliced
- 3 tbsp ground almonds
- 55 g/2 oz blanched pistachio nuts, finely chopped
- 2 tbsp chopped fresh coriander
- 2 tbsp chopped fresh mint
- salt
- toasted flaked almonds, to garnish
- naan bread, to serve

1 Heat a frying pan over a medium–low heat, then add the cardamom pods and dry-fry, stirring constantly, until you can smell the aroma. Immediately tip them out of the pan to prevent them burning. Repeat with the coriander seeds, cumin seeds, cinnamon, peppercorns and cloves. Put all the spices, except the cinnamon stick, in a spice grinder and grind to a powder.

2 Put the hot water and saffron threads in a small bowl and set aside.

3 Heat a large frying pan with a tight-fitting lid over a medium–high heat, then add the ghee. Add the onion and cook, stirring occasionally, for 5–8 minutes until golden brown. Add the garlic and ginger paste and continue stirring for a further 2 minutes.

4 Stir in the ground spices and the cinnamon stick. Remove from the heat and mix in the yogurt, a small amount at a time, stirring vigorously with each addition, then return to the heat and continue stirring for 2–3 minutes until the ghee separates. Add the chicken pieces.

5 Bring the mixture to the boil, stirring constantly, then reduce the heat to the lowest setting, cover the pan and simmer for 20 minutes, stirring occasionally and checking that the mixture isn't catching on the base of the pan. If it does start to catch, stir in a few tablespoons of water.

6 Stir the ground almonds, pistachio nuts, saffron liquid, half the coriander, all the mint and salt to taste into the chicken mixture. Re-cover the pan and continue simmering for about 5 minutes until the chicken is tender and the sauce is thickened. Sprinkle with the remaining coriander and the flaked almonds and serve hot with naan bread.

Chicken Tikka Masala

Serves 4–6

ingredients

- 400 g/14 oz canned chopped tomatoes
- 300 ml/10 fl oz double cream
- 1 cooked Tandoori Chicken (see page 53), cut into 8 pieces
- salt and pepper
- fresh chopped coriander, to garnish
- cooked basmati rice, to serve

tikka masala

- 25 g/1 oz ghee or 2 tbsp vegetable oil or groundnut oil
- 1 large garlic clove, finely chopped
- 1 fresh red chilli, deseeded and chopped
- 2 tsp ground cumin
- 2 tsp ground paprika
- ½ tsp salt
- pepper

1 To make the tikka masala, heat a large frying pan with a lid over a medium heat, then add the ghee. Add the garlic and chilli and stir-fry for 1 minute. Stir in the cumin, paprika, and salt and pepper to taste and continue stirring for about 30 seconds.

2 Stir the tomatoes and cream into the pan. Reduce the heat to low and leave to simmer for about 10 minutes, stirring frequently, until it reduces and thickens.

3 Meanwhile, remove all the bones and skin from the chicken pieces, then cut the meat into bite-sized pieces.

4 Adjust the seasoning of the sauce, if necessary. Add the chicken pieces to the pan, cover and leave to simmer for 3–5 minutes until the chicken is heated through. Garnish with coriander and serve immediately with rice.

Chicken Biryani

Serves 4–5

ingredients

- 85 g/3 oz natural yogurt
- 1 tbsp garlic purée
- 1 tbsp ginger purée
- 700 g/1 lb 9 oz skinless, boneless chicken thighs
- 1 tbsp white poppy seeds
- 2 tsp coriander seeds
- ½ mace blade
- 2 bay leaves, torn into small pieces
- ½ tsp black peppercorns
- 1 tsp green cardamom pods
- 2.5-cm/1-inch piece cinnamon stick, broken up
- 4 cloves
- 55 g/2 oz ghee or unsalted butter
- 1 large onion, finely sliced
- 1½ tsp salt, or to taste
- 2 tbsp sunflower oil and 1 onion, finely sliced, to garnish

rice

- pinch of saffron threads, pounded
- 2 tbsp hot milk
- 1½ tsp salt
- 2 x 5-cm/2-inch cinnamon sticks
- 3 star anise
- 2 bay leaves, crumbled
- 4 cloves
- 4 green cardamom pods, bruised
- 450 g/1 lb basmati rice, washed

1 Put the yogurt, garlic purée and ginger purée in a bowl and beat together with a fork until thoroughly blended. Put the chicken in a non-metallic bowl, add the yogurt mixture and mix until well coated. Cover and leave to marinate in the refrigerator for 2 hours.

2 Grind the next eight ingredients (all the seeds and spices) to a fine powder in a spice grinder and set aside. Heat a casserole large enough to hold the chicken and the rice together over a medium heat, then add the ghee. Add the onion and cook, stirring frequently, for 8–10 minutes until it has turned a medium brown colour. Reduce the heat to low, add the ground ingredients and cook, stirring, for 2–3 minutes. Add the marinated chicken and salt and cook, stirring, for 2 minutes. Turn off the heat and keep the chicken covered.

3 To make the rice, add the saffron to the hot milk and set aside to soak for 20 minutes. Preheat the oven to 180°C/350°F/Gas Mark 4. Bring a large saucepan of water to the boil and add the salt and spices. Add the rice, return to the boil and boil steadily for 2 minutes. Drain the rice, reserving the whole spices, and pile on top of the chicken. Pour the saffron and milk over the rice.

4 Soak a piece of greaseproof paper large enough to cover the top of the rice completely and squeeze out the excess water. Lay on top of the rice. Soak a clean tea towel, wring out and lay loosely on top of the greaseproof paper. Cover the casserole with a piece of foil. It is important to cover the rice in this way to contain all the steam inside the casserole, as the biryani cooks entirely in the vapour created inside the casserole. Put the lid on top and cook in the centre of the preheated oven for 1 hour. Turn off the oven and leave the rice to stand inside for 30 minutes.

5 Meanwhile, heat a small saucepan over a medium heat, then add the oil for the garnish. Add the onion and cook, stirring, for 12–15 minutes until browned.

6 Transfer the biryani to a warmed serving dish, garnish with the fried onions and serve immediately.

Chicken Breasts with
Coconut Milk

Serves 4

ingredients

- 1 small onion, chopped
- 1 fresh green chilli, deseeded and chopped
- 2.5-cm/1-inch piece fresh ginger, chopped
- 2 tsp ground coriander
- 1 tsp ground cumin
- 1 tsp fennel seeds
- 1 tsp ground star anise
- 1 tsp cardamom pods
- ½ tsp ground turmeric
- ½ tsp black peppercorns
- ½ tsp ground cloves
- 600 ml/1 pint canned coconut milk
- 4 skinless, boneless chicken breast portions
- vegetable oil, for brushing
- fresh coriander sprigs, to garnish

1 Place the onion, chilli, ginger, ground coriander, cumin, fennel seeds, star anise, cardamom pods, turmeric, peppercorns, cloves and 450 ml/16 fl oz of the coconut milk in a food processor and process to make a paste, adding more coconut milk if necessary.

2 Using a sharp knife, slash the chicken breasts several times and place in a large, shallow, non-metallic dish in a single layer. Pour over half the coconut milk mixture and turn to coat completely. Cover with clingfilm and leave to marinate in the refrigerator for at least 1 hour and up to 8 hours.

3 Heat a ridged griddle pan, then brush lightly with vegetable oil. Add the chicken, in batches if necessary, and cook for 6–7 minutes on each side, or until tender.

4 Meanwhile, pour the remaining coconut milk mixture into a saucepan and bring to the boil, stirring occasionally. Arrange the chicken on a warmed serving dish, spoon over a little of the coconut sauce and garnish with coriander sprigs. Serve hot.

Balti Chicken

Serves 6

ingredients

- 3 tbsp ghee or vegetable oil
- 2 large onions, sliced
- 3 tomatoes, sliced
- ½ tsp nigella seeds
- 4 black peppercorns
- 2 green cardamom pods
- 1 cinnamon stick
- 1 tsp chilli powder
- 1 tsp garam masala
- 2 tbsp Garlic and Ginger Paste (see page 15)
- 700 g/1 lb 9 oz skinless, boneless chicken breasts or thighs, diced
- 2 tbsp natural yogurt
- 2 tbsp chopped fresh coriander, plus extra sprigs to garnish
- 2 fresh green chillies, deseeded and finely chopped
- 2 tbsp lime juice
- salt

1 Heat a large, heavy-based frying pan over a low heat, then add the ghee. Add the onions and cook, stirring occasionally, for 10 minutes, or until golden. Add the tomatoes, nigella seeds, peppercorns, cardamom pods, cinnamon stick, chilli powder, garam masala and garlic and ginger paste, and season to taste with salt. Cook, stirring constantly, for 5 minutes.

2 Add the chicken and cook, stirring constantly, for 5 minutes, or until well coated in the spice paste. Stir in the yogurt. Cover and simmer, stirring occasionally, for 10 minutes.

3 Stir in the chopped coriander, chillies and lime juice. Transfer to a warmed serving dish, garnish with coriander sprigs and serve immediately.

Chicken Dopiaza

Serves 4

ingredients

- 700 g/1 lb 9 oz skinless, boneless chicken breasts or thighs
- juice of ½ lemon
- 1 tsp salt, or to taste
- 5 tbsp sunflower oil
- 2 large onions, roughly chopped
- 5 large garlic cloves, roughly chopped
- 2.5-cm/1-inch piece fresh ginger, roughly chopped
- 2 tbsp natural yogurt
- 2.5-cm/1-inch piece cinnamon stick, halved
- 4 green cardamom pods, bruised
- 4 cloves
- ½ tsp black peppercorns
- ½ tsp ground turmeric
- ½–1 tsp chilli powder
- 1 tsp ground coriander
- 4 tbsp passata
- 150 ml/5 fl oz lukewarm water
- ½ tsp granulated sugar
- 8 shallots, halved
- 1 tsp garam masala
- 2 tbsp chopped fresh coriander leaves
- 1 tomato, chopped
- naan bread, to serve

1 Cut the chicken into 2.5-cm/1-inch cubes and put in a non-metallic bowl. Add the lemon juice and half the salt and rub well into the chicken. Cover and leave to marinate in the refrigerator for 20 minutes.

2 Heat a small saucepan over a medium heat, then add 1 tablespoon of the oil. Add the onions, garlic and ginger and cook, stirring frequently, for 4–5 minutes. Remove from the heat and leave to cool slightly. Transfer the ingredients to a blender or food processor, add the yogurt and blend to a purée.

3 Heat 3 tablespoons of the remaining oil in a medium-sized, heavy-based saucepan over a low heat, add the cinnamon stick, cardamom pods, cloves and peppercorns and cook, stirring, for 25–30 seconds. Add the puréed ingredients, increase the heat to medium and cook, stirring frequently, for 5 minutes.

4 Add the turmeric, chilli powder and ground coriander and cook, stirring, for 2 minutes.

5 Add the passata and cook, stirring, for 3 minutes. Increase the heat slightly, then add the marinated chicken and cook, stirring, until it changes colour. Add the water, the remaining salt and the sugar. Bring to the boil, then reduce the heat to low, cover and cook for 10 minutes. Remove the lid and cook, uncovered, for a further 10 minutes, or until the sauce has thickened.

6 Meanwhile, heat the remaining oil in a small saucepan, add the shallots and stir-fry until browned and separated. Add the garam masala and cook, stirring, for 30 seconds. Stir the shallot mixture into the curry and simmer for 2 minutes. Stir in the fresh coriander and chopped tomato and remove from the heat. Serve immediately with naan bread.

Wok-cooked Chicken in
Tomato & Fenugreek Sauce

Serves 4

ingredients

- 700 g/1 lb 9 oz skinless, boneless chicken thighs, cut into 2.5-cm/1-inch cubes
- juice of 1 lime
- 1 tsp salt, or to taste
- 4 tbsp sunflower oil
- 1 large onion, finely chopped
- 2 tsp ginger purée
- 2 tsp garlic purée
- ½ tsp ground turmeric
- ½–1 tsp chilli powder
- 1 tbsp ground coriander
- 425 g/15 oz canned chopped tomatoes
- 125 ml/4 fl oz lukewarm water
- 1 tbsp dried fenugreek leaves
- ½ tsp garam masala
- 2 tbsp chopped fresh coriander leaves
- 2–4 fresh green chillies
- naan bread, to serve

1 Place the chicken in a non-metallic bowl and rub in the lime juice and salt. Cover and set aside for 30 minutes.

2 Heat a wok over a medium–high heat, then add the oil. Add the onion and stir-fry for 7–8 minutes until it begins to colour.

3 Add the ginger purée and garlic purée and continue to stir-fry for about a minute. Add the turmeric, chilli powder and ground coriander, then reduce the heat slightly and cook the spices for 25–30 seconds. Add half the tomatoes, stir-fry for 3–4 minutes, then add the remaining tomatoes. Continue to cook, stirring, until the tomato juice has evaporated and the oil separates from the spice paste and floats on the surface.

4 Add the chicken and increase the heat to high. Stir-fry for 4–5 minutes, then add the water, reduce the heat to medium-low and cook for 8–10 minutes, or until the sauce has thickened and the chicken is tender.

5 Add the fenugreek leaves, garam masala, half the coriander leaves and the chillies. Cook for 1–2 minutes, then remove from the heat and transfer to a serving plate. Garnish with the remaining coriander and serve immediately with naan bread.

Chicken in Green Chilli,
Mint & Coriander Sauce

Serves 4

ingredients

- 25 g/1 oz coriander leaves and stalks, roughly chopped
- 25 g/1 oz fresh spinach, roughly chopped
- 2.5-cm/1-inch piece fresh ginger, roughly chopped
- 3 garlic cloves, roughly chopped
- 2–3 fresh green chillies, roughly chopped
- 15 g/½ oz fresh mint leaves
- 1½ tbsp lemon juice
- 85 g/3 oz thick natural yogurt
- 4 tbsp sunflower oil
- 1 large onion, finely chopped
- 700 g/1 lb 9 oz skinless chicken thighs or breasts, cut into 2.5-cm/1-inch cubes
- 1 tsp ground turmeric
- ½ tsp sugar
- salt
- 1 small tomato, deseeded and cut into julienne strips, to garnish
- cooked basmati rice, to serve

1 Place the coriander, spinach, ginger, garlic, chillies, mint, lemon juice and ½ teaspoon of salt in a food processor or blender and process to a smooth purée. Add a little water, if necessary, to facilitate blade movement if using a blender. Remove and set aside.

2 Whisk the yogurt until smooth (otherwise it will curdle) and set aside.

3 Heat a wok over a medium–high heat, then add the oil. Add the onion and cook for 5–6 minutes, stirring frequently, until soft.

4 Add the chicken and stir-fry over a medium–high heat for 2–3 minutes until the meat turns opaque. Add the turmeric and sugar and salt to taste and stir-fry for a further 2 minutes, then reduce the heat to medium and add half the yogurt. Cook for 1 minute and add the remaining yogurt, then continue cooking over a medium heat until the yogurt resembles a thick batter and the oil is visible.

5 Add the puréed ingredients and cook for 4–5 minutes, stirring constantly. Remove from the heat and garnish with tomato strips. Serve immediately with rice.

Fried Chilli Chicken

Serves 4

ingredients
- 750 g/1 lb 10 oz chicken thighs
- 3 tbsp lemon juice
- 1 tsp salt, or to taste
- 5 large garlic cloves, roughly chopped
- 5-cm/2-inch piece fresh ginger, roughly chopped
- 1 medium onion, roughly chopped
- 2 fresh red chillies, roughly chopped
- 4 tbsp groundnut oil
- 1 tsp ground turmeric
- ½ tsp chilli powder
- 150 ml/5 fl oz lukewarm water
- 3–4 fresh green chillies
- cooked basmati rice, to serve

1 Put the chicken in a non-metallic bowl and rub in the lemon juice and salt. Set aside for 30 minutes.

2 Meanwhile, purée the garlic, ginger, onion and red chillies in a food processor or blender. Add a little water, if necessary, to facilitate blade movement if using a blender.

3 Heat a wide, shallow saucepan, preferably non-stick, over a medium–high heat, then add the oil. When the oil is hot, add the chicken in two batches and cook until golden brown on all sides. Lift out of the pan and drain on kitchen paper.

4 Add the puréed ingredients to the pan with the turmeric and chilli powder and reduce the heat to medium. Cook for 5–6 minutes, stirring regularly.

5 Add the chicken and water. Bring to the boil, reduce the heat to low, cover and cook for 20 minutes. Increase the heat to medium and cook for a further 8–10 minutes, stirring halfway through to ensure that the thickened sauce does not stick to the base of the pan.

6 Remove the lid and cook until the sauce is reduced to a paste-like consistency, stirring regularly to prevent the sauce sticking to the base of the pan. Add the green chillies and cook for 2–3 minutes, then remove from the heat and serve immediately with rice.

Vietnamese Chicken Curry

Serves 6

ingredients

- 2 lemon grass stalks
- 50 ml/2 fl oz vegetable oil
- 3 large garlic cloves, crushed
- 1 large shallot, thinly sliced
- 2 tbsp Indian curry powder
- 700 ml/1¼ pints coconut milk
- 500 ml/18 fl oz coconut water (not coconut milk) or chicken stock
- 2 tbsp fish sauce
- 4 fresh red bird's eye chillies or dried red Chinese (tien sien) chillies
- 6 kaffir lime leaves
- 6 boneless chicken thighs or breasts, 175–225 g/6–8 oz each, with or without skin, cut into 5-cm/2-inch pieces
- 1 large white yam or sweet potato, peeled and cut into 2.5-cm/1-inch chunks
- 2 Asian aubergines, cut into 2.5-cm/1-inch pieces
- 250 g/9 oz French beans, topped and tailed
- 2 carrots, peeled and cut diagonally into 1 cm/½ inch thick pieces
- fresh Thai basil sprigs, to garnish
- cooked jasmine rice, to serve

1 Discard the bruised leaves and root ends of the lemon grass stalks, then cut 15–20 cm/6–8 inches of the lower stalks into paper-thin slices.

2 Heat a wok over a high heat, then add the oil. Add the garlic and shallot and stir-fry for 5 minutes, or until golden. Add the lemon grass and curry powder and stir-fry for 2 minutes, or until fragrant. Add the coconut milk, coconut water, fish sauce, chillies and lime leaves and bring to the boil.

3 Reduce the heat to low and add the chicken, yam, aubergines, beans and carrots. Simmer, covered, for 1 hour, or until the chicken and vegetables are tender and the flavours have blended.

4 Serve immediately, garnished with Thai basil sprigs and accompanied by jasmine rice.

Thai Green Chicken Curry

Serves 4

ingredients

- 2 tbsp groundnut oil or sunflower oil
- 2 tbsp Thai Green Curry Paste (see page 14)
- 500 g/1 lb 2 oz skinless, boneless chicken breasts, cut into cubes
- 2 kaffir lime leaves, roughly torn
- 1 lemon grass stalk, finely chopped
- 225 ml/8 fl oz coconut milk
- 16 baby aubergines, halved
- 2 tbsp fish sauce
- fresh Thai basil sprigs and thinly sliced kaffir lime leaves, to garnish

1 Heat a wok over a medium–high heat, then add the oil. Add the curry paste and stir-fry briefly until all the aromas are released.

2 Add the chicken, lime leaves and lemon grass and stir-fry for 3–4 minutes until the meat is beginning to colour. Add the coconut milk and aubergines and simmer gently for 8–10 minutes, or until tender.

3 Stir in the fish sauce and serve immediately, garnished with basil sprigs and lime leaves.

Chicken & Peanut Curry

Serves 4

ingredients

- 1 tbsp vegetable oil or groundnut oil
- 2 red onions, sliced
- 2 tbsp Penang Curry Paste (see page 15)
- 400 ml/14 fl oz coconut milk
- 150 ml/¼ pint chicken stock
- 4 kaffir lime leaves, coarsely torn
- 1 lemon grass stalk, finely chopped
- 6 skinned, boned chicken thighs, chopped
- 1 tbsp fish sauce
- 2 tbsp Thai soy sauce
- 1 tsp palm sugar or soft light brown sugar
- 50 g/1¾ oz unsalted peanuts, roasted and chopped, plus extra to garnish
- 175 g/6 oz fresh pineapple, coarsely chopped
- 15-cm/6-inch piece cucumber, peeled, deseeded and thickly sliced, plus extra to garnish

1 Heat a wok over a medium–high heat, then add the oil. Add the onions and stir-fry for 1 minute. Add the curry paste and stir-fry for 1–2 minutes.

2 Pour in the coconut milk and stock. Add the lime leaves and lemon grass and simmer for 1 minute. Add the chicken and gradually bring to the boil. Simmer for 8–10 minutes until the chicken is tender.

3 Stir in the fish sauce, soy sauce and sugar and simmer for 1–2 minutes. Stir in the peanuts, pineapple and cucumber and cook for 30 seconds. Serve immediately, garnished with extra nuts and cucumber.

Shredded Chicken & Mixed
Mushrooms

Serves 4

ingredients

- 2 tbsp vegetable oil or groundnut oil
- 2 skinless, boneless chicken breasts
- 1 red onion, sliced
- 2 garlic cloves, finely chopped
- 2.5-cm/1-inch piece fresh ginger, grated
- 115 g/4 oz baby button mushrooms
- 115 g/4 oz shiitake mushrooms, halved
- 115 g/4 oz chestnut mushrooms, sliced
- 2–3 tbsp Thai Green Curry Paste (see page 14)
- 2 tbsp Thai soy sauce
- 4 tbsp chopped fresh parsley
- cooked noodles, to serve

1 Heat a wok over a medium heat, then add the oil. Add the chicken and cook on all sides until lightly browned and cooked through. Remove with a slotted spoon, shred into even-sized pieces and set aside.

2 Pour off any excess oil, then add the onion, garlic and ginger and stir-fry for 1–2 minutes until soft. Add the mushrooms and stir-fry for 2–3 minutes until they start to brown.

3 Add the curry paste, soy sauce and shredded chicken to the wok and stir-fry for 1–2 minutes. Stir in the parsley and serve immediately with noodles.

Thai Yellow Chicken Curry

Serves 4

ingredients

- 2 tbsp vegetable oil or groundnut oil
- 2 onions, cut into thin wedges
- 2 garlic cloves, finely chopped
- 2 skinless, boneless chicken breasts, cut into strips
- 175 g/6 oz baby corn, halved lengthways

spice paste

- 6 tbsp Thai Yellow Curry Paste (see page 14)
- 150 ml/5 fl oz natural yogurt
- 400 ml/14 fl oz water
- handful of fresh coriander, chopped
- handful of fresh Thai basil leaves, shredded, plus extra sprigs to garnish

1 To make the spice paste, heat a wok over a medium heat, then add the curry paste and stir-fry for 2–3 minutes. Stir in the yogurt, water and herbs, bring to the boil and simmer for 2–3 minutes.

2 Meanwhile, heat a separate wok over a medium–high heat, then add the oil. Add the onions and garlic and stir-fry for 2–3 minutes. Add the chicken and corn and stir-fry for 3–4 minutes until the meat and corn are tender.

3 Stir in the spice paste and bring to the boil. Simmer for 2–3 minutes until heated through. Serve immediately, garnished with basil sprigs.

Cumin-scented
Chicken Curry

Serves 4

ingredients

- 700 g/1 lb 9 oz boneless chicken thighs or breasts, cut into 5-cm/2-inch pieces
- juice of 1 lime
- 1 tsp salt, or to taste
- 3 tbsp sunflower oil
- 1 tsp cumin seeds
- 2.5-cm/1-inch piece cinnamon stick
- 5 green cardamom pods, bruised
- 4 cloves
- 1 large onion, finely chopped
- 2 tsp garlic purée
- 2 tsp ginger purée
- ½ tsp ground turmeric
- 2 tsp ground cumin
- ½ tsp chilli powder
- 225 g/8 oz canned chopped tomatoes
- 1 tbsp tomato purée
- ½ tsp sugar
- 225 ml/8 fl oz lukewarm water
- ½ tsp garam masala
- 2 tbsp chopped fresh coriander leaves, plus extra sprigs to garnish
- naan bread, to serve

1 Put the chicken in a non-metallic bowl and rub in the lime juice and salt. Cover and set aside for 30 minutes.

2 Heat a wok over a low heat, then add the oil. Add the cumin seeds, cinnamon, cardamom pods and cloves. Leave them to sizzle for 25–30 seconds, then add the onion. Cook, stirring frequently, for 5 minutes, or until the onion is soft.

3 Add the garlic purée and ginger purée and cook for about a minute, then add the turmeric, ground cumin and chilli powder. Add the tomatoes, tomato purée and sugar. Cook over a medium heat, stirring regularly, until the tomatoes reach a paste-like consistency and the oil separates from the paste. Sprinkle over a little water if the mixture sticks to the wok.

4 Add the chicken and increase the heat to medium–high. Stir until the chicken changes colour, then pour in the water. Bring to the boil, reduce the heat to medium–low and cook for 12–15 minutes, or until the sauce has thickened and the chicken is tender.

5 Stir in the garam masala and chopped coriander. Transfer to a serving dish and garnish with coriander sprigs. Serve immediately with naan bread.

Tandoori Chicken

Serves 4

ingredients

- 1 chicken, weighing
  1.5 kg/3 lb 5 oz, skinned
- ½ lemon
- 1 tsp salt
- 25 g/1 oz ghee, melted
- fresh coriander sprigs, to garnish
- cooked basmati rice and lemon
  wedges, to serve

tandoori masala paste

- 1 tbsp Garlic and Ginger Paste
  (see page 15)
- 1 tbsp ground paprika
- 1 tsp ground cinnamon
- 1 tsp ground cumin
- ½ tsp ground coriander
- ¼ tsp chilli powder, ideally
  Kashmiri chilli powder
- pinch of ground cloves
- ¼ tsp red food colouring
  (optional)
- few drops of yellow food
  colouring (optional)
- 200 ml/7 fl oz natural yogurt

1 To make the tandoori masala paste, combine the garlic and ginger paste, dry spices and food colouring, if using, in a bowl and stir in the yogurt. The paste can be used immediately or stored in an airtight container in the refrigerator for up to 3 days.

2 Use a small knife to make thin cuts all over the chicken. Rub the lemon half over the chicken, then rub the salt into the cuts. Put the chicken in a deep, non-metallic bowl, add the paste and use your hands to rub it all over the bird and into the cuts. Cover the bowl with clingfilm and refrigerate for at least 4 hours, but ideally up to 24 hours.

3 When you are ready to cook the chicken, preheat the oven to 200°C/400°F/Gas Mark 6. Put the chicken on a rack in a roasting tin, breast-side up, and drizzle over the melted ghee. Roast in the preheated oven for 45 minutes, then quickly remove the bird from the oven in the tin and increase the temperature to its highest setting.

4 Very carefully pour out any fat from the bottom of the tin. Return the chicken to the oven and roast for a further 10–15 minutes until the juices run clear when you pierce the thigh with a knife and the paste is lightly charred.

5 Leave to stand for 10 minutes, then garnish with coriander sprigs and serve with rice and lemon wedges.

Sri Lankan Chicken Curry

Serves 4

ingredients

- 700 g/1 lb 9 oz skinless, boneless chicken thighs or breasts
- 1 tsp salt, or to taste
- 2 tbsp white wine vinegar
- 2 tsp coriander seeds
- 1 tsp cumin seeds
- 2.5-cm/1-inch piece cinnamon stick, broken up
- 4 cloves
- 4 green cardamom pods
- 6 fenugreek seeds
- 4 dried red chillies, torn into pieces
- 10–12 curry leaves
- 4 tbsp sunflower oil
- 1 large onion, finely chopped
- 2 tsp ginger purée
- 2 tsp garlic purée
- 1 tsp ground turmeric
- ½ tsp chilli powder
- 1 lemon grass stalk, finely sliced
- 200 g/7 oz canned chopped tomatoes
- 150 ml/5 fl oz lukewarm water
- 55 g/2 oz creamed coconut, cut into small pieces
- cooked basmati rice, to serve

1 Cut the chicken into 5-cm/2-inch chunks and put them in a non-metallic bowl. Add the salt and vinegar, mix well and set aside for 30 minutes.

2 Heat a small, heavy-based saucepan over a medium heat, then add the coriander seeds, cumin seeds, cinnamon, cloves, cardamom pods, fenugreek, chillies and curry leaves and dry-roast until they are dark, but not black. Remove and leave to cool, then grind in a spice grinder until finely ground. Set aside.

3 Heat a wok over a medium heat, then add the oil. Add the onion and cook for 5 minutes until translucent. Add the ginger purée and garlic purée and continue to cook for a further 2 minutes.

4 Add the turmeric, chilli powder, chicken and the ground spice mix. Stir and mix well, then add the lemon grass, tomatoes and water. Bring to the boil, reduce the heat to low, cover the wok and cook for 25 minutes.

5 Add the coconut and stir until it has dissolved. Cook for 7–8 minutes, then remove from the heat and serve immediately with rice.

Turkey & Aubergine Curry

Serves 4

ingredients

- 2 tsp sunflower oil
- 1 onion, chopped
- 2 garlic cloves, crushed
- 1–2 fresh serrano chillies, deseeded and chopped
- 1 tsp ground cumin
- 1 tsp ground coriander
- ½ tsp turmeric
- 1 small aubergine, about 225 g/8 oz, trimmed and cut into small cubes
- 225 g/8 oz skinless, boneless turkey breast, cut into cubes
- 2 carrots, about 175 g/6 oz, peeled and chopped
- 1 small red pepper, deseeded and chopped
- 450 ml/16 fl oz chicken stock
- 1 tbsp chopped fresh coriander, to garnish

1 Heat a wok over a medium heat, then add the oil. Add the onion, garlic and chillies and cook, stirring, for 2 minutes. Sprinkle in all of the spices and cook, stirring constantly, for a further 2 minutes.

2 Add the aubergine and turkey and cook, stirring, for 5 minutes, or until the turkey is browned all over. Add the carrots and red pepper, stir, then pour in the stock. Bring to the boil, cover with a lid and simmer for 20–25 minutes, or until the turkey is tender.

3 Sprinkle with chopped coriander and serve immediately, divided equally between four warmed bowls.

Duck Jungle Curry

Serves 4

ingredients
- 2 tbsp groundnut oil
- 6 tbsp Thai Green Curry Paste (see page 14)
- 1 tbsp finely chopped galangal or ginger root
- 4 tbsp finely chopped shallots
- 2 tbsp fish sauce
- 500 ml/18 fl oz chicken stock
- 350 g/12 oz boneless, skinless duck meat, thinly sliced into small strips
- 150 g/5½ oz baby aubergines, quartered
- 2 small yellow courgettes, thickly sliced diagonally
- 225 g/8 oz can sliced bamboo shoots, drained and rinsed
- juice of 1 lime
- handful of Thai basil leaves
- cooked jasmine rice, to serve

1 Heat a wok over a medium–high heat, then add the oil. Add the curry paste, galangal and shallots and stir-fry for 1 minute until fragrant. Add the fish sauce and stock, and bring to the boil.

2 Add the duck, aubergines and courgettes, and simmer for about 3 minutes until the vegetables have softened slightly. Add the remaining ingredients and simmer for a few more minutes until the duck is tender.

3 Serve immediately in individual bowls, accompanied with rice.

Chapter 2
Meat

Beef Madras

Serves 4

ingredients

- 1–2 dried red chillies
- 2 tsp ground coriander
- 2 tsp ground turmeric
- 1 tsp black mustard seeds
- ½ tsp ground ginger
- ¼ tsp pepper
- 140 g/5 oz creamed coconut, grated, dissolved in 300 ml/ 10 fl oz boiling water
- 55 g/2 oz ghee or 4 tbsp vegetable oil or groundnut oil
- 2 onions, chopped
- 3 large garlic cloves, chopped
- 700 g/1 lb 9 oz lean stewing steak, trimmed and cut into 5-cm/2-inch cubes
- 250 ml/9 fl oz beef stock
- lemon juice
- salt
- poppadoms, to serve

1 Chop the chillies and put them in a small bowl with the coriander, turmeric, mustard seeds, ginger and pepper. Stir in a little of the dissolved creamed coconut to make a thin paste.

2 Heat a large frying pan with a tight-fitting lid or a flameproof casserole over a medium–high heat, then add the ghee. Add the onions and garlic and cook for 5–8 minutes, stirring frequently, until the onions are golden brown. Add the spice paste and stir for 2 minutes, or until you can smell the aromas.

3 Add the meat and stock and bring to the boil. Reduce the heat to its lowest level, cover tightly and simmer for 1½ hours, or until the beef is tender. Check occasionally that the meat isn't catching on the base of the pan and stir in a little extra water or stock, if necessary.

4 Uncover the pan and stir in the remaining dissolved coconut cream with the lemon juice and salt to taste. Bring to the boil, stirring, then reduce the heat again and simmer, still uncovered, until the sauce reduces slightly. Serve immediately with some poppadoms on the side.

Beef Korma with Almonds

Serves 6

ingredients
- 300 ml/10 fl oz vegetable oil
- 3 onions, finely chopped
- 1 kg/2 lb 4 oz lean beef, cubed
- 1½ tsp garam masala
- 1½ tsp ground coriander
- 1½ tsp finely chopped fresh ginger
- 1½ tsp crushed fresh garlic
- 1 tsp salt
- 150 ml/5 fl oz natural yogurt
- 2 whole cloves
- 3 green cardamom pods
- 4 black peppercorns
- 600 ml/1 pint water
- chapattis, to serve

to garnish
- chopped blanched almonds
- sliced fresh green chillies
- chopped fresh coriander

1 Heat a frying pan over a medium–high heat, then add the oil. Add the onions and stir-fry for 8–10 minutes until golden. Remove half the onions and reserve.

2 Add the meat to the remaining onions in the pan and stir-fry for 5 minutes. Remove the pan from the heat.

3 Mix the garam masala, ground coriander, ginger, garlic, salt and yogurt together in a large bowl. Gradually add the meat to the yogurt and spice mixture and mix to coat the meat on all sides. Place the meat mixture in the pan, return to the heat, and stir-fry for 5–7 minutes, or until the mixture is nearly brown.

4 Add the cloves, cardamom pods and peppercorns. Add the water, reduce the heat, cover and simmer for 45–60 minutes. If the water has completely evaporated, but the meat is still not tender enough, add another 300 ml/10 fl oz water and cook for a further 10–15 minutes, stirring occasionally. Transfer to serving dishes and garnish with the reserved onions, chopped almonds, chillies and fresh coriander. Serve immediately with chapattis.

Balti Beef

Serves 4–6

ingredients

- 25 g/1 oz ghee or 2 tbsp vegetable oil or groundnut oil
- 1 large onion, chopped
- 2 garlic cloves, crushed
- 2 large red peppers, deseeded and chopped
- 600 g/1 lb 5 oz boneless beef, such as sirloin, thinly sliced
- fresh coriander sprigs, to garnish
- naan bread, to serve

balti sauce

- 25 g/1 oz ghee or 2 tbsp vegetable oil or groundnut oil
- 2 large onions, chopped
- 1 tbsp Garlic and Ginger Paste (see page 15)
- 400 g/14 oz canned chopped tomatoes
- 1 tsp ground paprika
- ½ tsp ground turmeric
- ½ tsp ground cumin
- ½ tsp ground coriander
- ¼ tsp chilli powder
- ¼ tsp ground cardamom
- 1 bay leaf
- salt and pepper

1 To make the balti sauce, heat a wok over a medium–high heat, then add the ghee and melt. Add the onions and garlic and ginger paste and stir-fry for about 5 minutes until the onion is golden brown. Stir in the tomatoes, then add the paprika, turmeric, cumin, coriander, chilli powder, cardamom and bay leaf and salt and pepper to taste. Bring to the boil, stirring, then reduce the heat and simmer for 20 minutes, stirring occasionally.

2 Leave the sauce to cool slightly, then remove the bay leaf and pour the mixture into a food processor or blender and process to a smooth sauce.

3 Wipe out the wok and return it to a medium–high heat. Add the ghee and melt. Add the onion and garlic and stir-fry for 5–8 minutes until golden brown. Add the red peppers and continue stir-frying for 2 minutes.

4 Stir in the beef and continue stirring for 2 minutes until it starts to turn brown. Add the balti sauce and bring to the boil. Reduce the heat and simmer for 5 minutes, or until the sauce slightly reduces and the meat is tender. Adjust the seasoning, if necessary. Garnish with coriander sprigs and serve immediately with naan bread.

Coconut Beef Curry

Serves 4

ingredients

- 1 tbsp ground coriander
- 1 tbsp ground cumin
- 3 tbsp Masaman Curry Paste
  (see page 15)
- 150 ml/5 fl oz water
- 75 g/2¾ oz creamed coconut
- 450 g/1 lb beef fillet,
  cut into strips
- 400 ml/14 fl oz coconut milk
- 50 g/1¾ oz unsalted peanuts,
  finely chopped
- 2 tbsp fish sauce
- 1 tsp palm sugar or soft light
  brown sugar
- 4 kaffir lime leaves
- fresh coriander sprigs, to garnish
- cooked jasmine rice, to serve

1 Combine the coriander, cumin and curry paste in a bowl. Pour the water into a saucepan, add the creamed coconut and heat until it has dissolved. Add the curry paste mixture and simmer for 1 minute.

2 Add the beef and simmer for 6–8 minutes, then add the coconut milk, peanuts, fish sauce and sugar. Simmer gently for 15–20 minutes until the meat is tender.

3 Add the lime leaves and simmer for 1–2 minutes. Garnish with coriander sprigs and serve immediately with rice.

Beef Rendang

Serves 4

ingredients

- 5–6 dried red chillies
- 2–3 fresh red chillies, roughly chopped
- 4–5 shallots or 1 large onion, roughly chopped
- 4 large garlic cloves, roughly chopped
- 2.5-cm/1-inch piece fresh ginger, roughly chopped
- 2 tbsp water
- 1 tsp coriander seeds
- 1 tsp cumin seeds
- 55 g/2 oz desiccated coconut
- 4 tbsp groundnut oil
- 700 g/1 lb 9 oz prime-quality casserole beef, trimmed and cut into 2.5-cm/1-inch cubes
- 1 tbsp dark soy sauce
- 1 lemon grass stalk, finely chopped
- 3 kaffir lime leaves, shredded, plus extra to garnish
- ½ tsp salt
- 200 ml/7 fl oz lukewarm water
- 1 tbsp tamarind juice
- 400 ml/14 fl oz coconut milk
- toasted flaked coconut, to garnish
- cooked jasmine rice, to serve

1 Soak the dried chillies in boiling water for 10 minutes, then drain and place in a food processor or blender. Add the fresh chillies, shallots, garlic, ginger and water, and blend until the ingredients are smooth.

2 Heat a small, heavy-based saucepan over a medium heat and add the coriander and cumin seeds. Stir for about a minute until they release their aroma, then remove them from the pan and let cool. In the same pan, dry-roast the desiccated coconut, stirring constantly, until it is tinged with a light brown colour. Remove from the pan and cool, then mix the coconut with the roasted spices, and grind them in two batches in a spice grinder.

3 Heat a medium-sized saucepan over a medium heat, then add the oil. Add the puréed ingredients and cook, stirring regularly, for 5–6 minutes. Add a little water to prevent the mixture sticking and continue to cook for a further 5–6 minutes, adding water if necessary.

4 Add the meat and increase the heat to medium–high. Stir until the meat changes colour, and add the roasted coconut mixture, soy sauce, lemon grass, lime leaves and salt. Stir and mix well and pour in the water. Bring to the boil, reduce the heat to low, then cover and simmer for 45 minutes, stirring occasionally to ensure that the mixture does not stick to the base of the pan.

5 Add the tamarind juice and coconut milk, bring to a gentle simmer, cover and cook for a further 45 minutes, or until the meat is tender. Remove the lid and cook over a medium heat, if necessary, to thicken the sauce. Garnish with the toasted coconut and shredded lime leaves and serve immediately with rice.

Masaman Curry

Serves 4

ingredients

- 2 tbsp groundnut oil or vegetable oil
- 225 g/8 oz shallots, roughly chopped
- 1 garlic clove, crushed
- 450 g/1 lb beef fillet, thickly sliced and then cut into 2.5-cm/1-inch cubes
- 2 tbsp Masaman Curry Paste (see page 15)
- 3 potatoes, cut into 2.5-cm/ 1-inch cubes
- 400 ml/14 fl oz coconut milk
- 2 tbsp soy sauce
- 150 ml/5 fl oz beef stock
- 1 tsp palm sugar or soft light brown sugar
- 85 g/3 oz unsalted peanuts
- handful of fresh coriander, chopped
- cooked noodles, to serve

1 Heat a wok over a medium–high heat, then add the oil. Add the shallots and garlic and stir-fry for 1–2 minutes until soft. Add the beef and curry paste and stir-fry over a high heat for 2–3 minutes until browned all over. Add the potatoes, coconut milk, soy sauce, stock and sugar and bring gently to the boil, stirring occasionally. Reduce the heat and simmer for 8–10 minutes until the potatoes are tender.

2 Meanwhile, heat a separate wok over a medium–high heat, add the peanuts and cook, shaking the wok frequently, for 2–3 minutes until lightly browned. Add to the curry with the coriander and stir well. Serve hot with noodles.

Kheema Matar

Serves 4–6

ingredients

- 25 g/1 oz ghee or 2 tbsp vegetable oil or groundnut oil
- 2 tsp cumin seeds
- 1 large onion, finely chopped
- 1 tbsp Garlic and Ginger Paste (see page 15)
- 2 bay leaves
- 1 tsp mild, medium or hot curry powder, to taste
- 2 tomatoes, deseeded and chopped
- 1 tsp ground coriander
- ¼–½ tsp chilli powder
- ¼ tsp ground turmeric
- pinch of sugar
- ½ tsp salt
- ½ tsp pepper
- 500 g/1 lb 2 oz lean minced beef or lamb
- 250 g/9 oz frozen peas, straight from the freezer

1 Heat a large frying pan with a tight-fitting lid or a flameproof casserole over a medium–high heat, then add the ghee. Add the cumin seeds and cook, stirring, for 30 seconds, or until they start to crackle.

2 Stir in the onion, garlic and ginger paste, bay leaves and curry powder and continue to stir-fry until the fat separates.

3 Stir in the tomatoes and cook for 1–2 minutes. Stir in the coriander, chilli powder, turmeric, sugar, salt and pepper and stir for 30 seconds.

4 Add the beef, using a wooden spoon to break it up, and cook for 5 minutes, or until the meat is no longer pink. Reduce the heat and simmer, stirring occasionally, for 10 minutes.

5 Add the peas and continue simmering for a further 10–15 minutes until the peas are thawed and hot. If there is too much liquid left in the pan, increase the heat and leave it to bubble for a few minutes until it reduces. Serve immediately.

Lamb Rogan Josh

Serves 4

ingredients
- 350 ml/12 fl oz natural yogurt
- ½ tsp ground asafoetida, dissolved in 2 tbsp water
- 700 g/1 lb 9 oz boneless leg of lamb, trimmed and cut into 5-cm/2-inch cubes
- 2 tomatoes, deseeded and chopped
- 1 onion, chopped
- 25 g/1 oz ghee or 2 tbsp vegetable oil or groundnut oil
- 1½ tbsp Garlic and Ginger Paste (see page 15)
- 2 tbsp tomato purée
- 2 bay leaves
- 1 tbsp ground coriander
- ¼–1 tsp chilli powder, ideally Kashmiri chilli powder
- ½ tsp ground turmeric
- 1 tsp salt
- ½ tsp garam masala
- bay leaf, to garnish

1 Put the yogurt in a large, non-metallic bowl and stir in the dissolved asafoetida. Add the lamb and use your hands to rub in all the marinade, then set aside for 30 minutes.

2 Meanwhile, put the tomatoes and onion in a blender and process until blended.

3 Heat a large frying pan with a tight-fitting lid or a flameproof casserole over a medium heat, then add the ghee. Add the garlic and ginger paste and stir until the aromas are released. Stir in the tomato mixture, tomato purée, bay leaves, coriander, chilli powder and turmeric, reduce the heat to low and simmer, stirring occasionally, for 5–8 minutes.

4 Add the lamb and salt with any leftover marinade and stir for 2 minutes. Cover, reduce the heat to low and simmer, stirring occasionally, for 30 minutes. The lamb should give off enough moisture to prevent it catching on the base of the pan, but if the sauce looks too dry, stir in a little water.

5 Sprinkle with the garam masala, re-cover the pan and continue simmering for 15–20 minutes, or until the lamb is tender. Serve immediately, garnished with a bay leaf.

Lamb Dhansak

Serves 4–6

ingredients

- 700 g/1 lb 9 oz boneless shoulder of lamb, trimmed and cut into 5-cm/2-inch cubes
- 1 tbsp Garlic and Ginger Paste (see page 15)
- 5 green cardamom pods
- 200 g/7 oz yellow lentils (toor dal)
- 100 g/3½ oz pumpkin, peeled, deseeded and chopped
- 1 carrot, thinly sliced
- 1 fresh green chilli, deseeded and chopped
- 1 tsp fenugreek powder
- 500 ml/18 fl oz water
- 1 large onion, thinly sliced
- 25 g/1 oz ghee or 2 tbsp vegetable oil or groundnut oil
- 2 garlic cloves, crushed
- salt
- chopped fresh coriander, to garnish

dhansak masala

- 1 tsp garam masala
- ½ tsp ground coriander
- ½ tsp ground cumin
- ½ tsp chilli powder
- ½ tsp ground turmeric
- ¼ tsp ground cardamom
- ¼ tsp ground cloves

1 Put the lamb and 1 teaspoon of salt in a large saucepan with enough water to cover and bring to the boil. Reduce the heat and simmer, skimming the surface as necessary until no more foam rises. Stir in the garlic and ginger paste and cardamom pods and continue simmering for a total of 30 minutes.

2 Meanwhile, put the lentils, pumpkin, carrot, chilli and fenugreek powder in a large heavy-based saucepan and pour over the water. Bring to the boil, stirring occasionally, then reduce the heat and simmer for 20–30 minutes until the lentils and carrot are very tender. Stir in a little extra water if the lentils look as though they will catch on the base of the pan.

3 Leave the lentil mixture to cool slightly, then pour it into a food processor or blender and process until a thick, smooth sauce forms.

4 While the lamb and lentils are cooking, put the onion in a bowl, sprinkle with 1 teaspoon of salt and leave to stand for about 5 minutes to extract the moisture. Squeeze out the moisture using your hands.

5 Heat a large frying pan with a tight-fitting lid or a flameproof casserole over a high heat, then add the ghee. Add the onion and cook, stirring constantly, for 2 minutes. Remove one third of the onion and reserve, then continue frying the remainder for a further 1–2 minutes until golden brown. Use a slotted spoon to remove the onion from the pan immediately, as it will continue to darken as it cools.

6 Return the reserved onion to the pan with the garlic. Stir in all the dhansak masala ingredients and cook for 2 minutes, stirring constantly. Add the cooked lamb and stir for a further 2 minutes. Add the lentil sauce and simmer over a medium heat to warm through, stirring and adding a little extra water, if needed. Adjust the seasoning, if necessary. Sprinkle with the remaining onion and serve immediately, garnished with coriander.

Lamb Pasanda

Serves 4–6

ingredients

- 600 g/1 lb 5 oz boneless shoulder or leg of lamb
- 2 tbsp Garlic and Ginger Paste (see page 15)
- 55 g/2 oz ghee or 4 tbsp vegetable oil or groundnut oil
- 3 large onions, chopped
- 1 fresh green chilli, deseeded and chopped
- 2 green cardamom pods, bruised
- 1 cinnamon stick, broken in half
- 2 tsp ground coriander
- 1 tsp ground cumin
- 1 tsp ground turmeric
- 250 ml/9 fl oz water
- 150 ml/5 fl oz double cream
- 4 tbsp ground almonds
- 1½ tsp salt
- 1 tsp garam masala
- paprika and toasted flaked almonds, to garnish

1 Cut the meat into thin slices, then place the slices between clingfilm and pound with a rolling pin or meat mallet to make them even thinner. Put the lamb slices in a non-metallic bowl, add the garlic and ginger paste and use your hands to rub the paste into the lamb. Cover and set aside in a cool place to marinate for 2 hours.

2 Heat a large frying pan with a tight-fitting lid over a medium–high heat, then add the ghee. Add the onions and chilli and cook, stirring frequently, for 5–8 minutes until the onions are golden brown.

3 Stir in the cardamom pods, cinnamon stick, coriander, cumin and turmeric and continue stirring for 2 minutes, or until the spices are aromatic.

4 Add the meat to the pan and cook, stirring occasionally, for about 5 minutes until it is brown on all sides and the fat begins to separate. Stir in the water and bring to the boil, still stirring. Reduce the heat to its lowest setting, cover the pan tightly and simmer for 40 minutes, or until the meat is tender.

5 When the lamb is tender, stir the cream and ground almonds together in a bowl. Beat in 6 tablespoons of the cooking liquid from the pan, then gradually beat this mixture back into the pan. Stir in the salt and garam masala. Simmer for a further 5 minutes, uncovered, stirring occasionally.

6 Garnish with paprika and toasted flaked almonds and serve immediately.

Peshawar-style Lamb Curry

Serves 4

ingredients
- 4 tbsp sunflower oil
- 2.5-cm/1-inch piece cinnamon stick
- 5 green cardamom pods, bruised
- 5 cloves
- 2 bay leaves
- 700 g/1 lb 9 oz boneless leg of lamb, cut into 2.5-cm/1-inch cubes
- 1 large onion, finely chopped
- 2 tsp ginger purée
- 2 tsp garlic purée
- 1 tbsp tomato purée
- 1 tsp ground turmeric
- 1 tsp ground coriander
- 1 tsp ground cumin
- 125 g/4½ oz thick natural yogurt
- 2 tsp gram flour or cornflour
- ½–1 tsp chilli powder
- 150 ml/5 fl oz lukewarm water
- 1 tbsp chopped fresh mint leaves
- 2 tbsp chopped fresh coriander leaves
- naan bread, to serve

1 Heat a medium-sized saucepan over a low heat, then add the oil. Add the cinnamon, cardamom pods, cloves and bay leaves. Leave to sizzle for 25–30 seconds, then add the meat, increase the heat to medium–high and cook until the meat begins to brown and all the natural juices have evaporated.

2 Add the onion, ginger purée and garlic purée, cook for 5–6 minutes, stirring regularly, then add the tomato purée, turmeric, ground coriander and cumin. Continue to cook for 3–4 minutes.

3 Whisk together the yogurt, gram flour and chilli powder and add to the meat. Reduce the heat to low, add the water, cover and simmer, stirring to ensure that the sauce does not stick to the base of the pan, for 45–50 minutes, or until the meat is tender. Simmer, uncovered, to thicken the sauce to the desired consistency.

4 Stir in the fresh mint and coriander, remove from the heat and serve immediately with naan bread.

Lamb, Tomato & Aubergine Curry

Serves 4

ingredients

- 2 tbsp sunflower oil
- 500 g/1 lb 2 oz lamb fillet or leg, cut into cubes
- 1 large onion, coarsely chopped
- 2–3 tbsp curry paste
- 1 aubergine, cut into small cubes
- 10 tomatoes, peeled, deseeded and coarsely chopped
- 400 ml/14 fl oz coconut milk
- 300 ml/10 fl oz lamb stock
- 2 tbsp chopped fresh coriander, plus extra sprigs to garnish
- naan bread, to serve

1 Heat a wok over a medium–high heat, then add the oil. Add the lamb in batches and cook for 8–10 minutes, or until browned all over. Remove with a slotted spoon and reserve.

2 Add the onion to the wok and cook for 2–3 minutes, or until just soft. Add the curry paste and stir-fry for a further 2 minutes. Add the aubergine, three quarters of the tomatoes and the lamb and stir together.

3 Add the coconut milk and stock and simmer gently for 30–40 minutes until the lamb is tender and the curry has thickened.

4 Mix the remaining tomatoes and the chopped coriander together in a small bowl, then stir into the curry. Garnish with sprigs of coriander and serve immediately with naan bread.

Lamb in Cinnamon-scented
Fenugreek Sauce

Serves 4

ingredients

- 700 g/1 lb 9 oz boneless leg or neck end of lamb, cut into 2.5-cm/1-inch cubes
- 4 tbsp red wine vinegar
- 1 tsp salt, or to taste
- 4 tbsp sunflower oil
- 5-cm/2-inch piece cinnamon stick, halved
- 5 green cardamom pods, bruised
- 5 cloves
- 1 large onion, finely chopped
- 2 tsp ginger purée
- 2 tsp garlic purée
- 2 tsp ground cumin
- 1 tsp ground turmeric
- ½–1 tsp chilli powder
- 225 g/8 oz canned chopped tomatoes
- 1½ tbsp dried fenugreek leaves
- 175 ml/6 fl oz lukewarm water
- 2 tsp ghee or unsalted butter
- ½ tsp garam masala
- fresh coriander sprigs, to garnish
- cooked basmati rice, to serve

1 Put the meat in a non-metallic bowl and rub in the vinegar and salt. Set aside for 30–40 minutes.

2 Heat a medium-sized, heavy-based saucepan over a low heat, then add oil. Add the cinnamon, cardamom pods and cloves. Let them sizzle for 25–30 seconds, then add the onion, increase the heat to medium and cook, stirring regularly, until the onion is soft but not brown.

3 Add the ginger purée and garlic purée and cook for a further 2–3 minutes, then add the cumin, turmeric and chilli powder. Cook for 1–2 minutes and add the tomatoes. Increase the heat slightly and continue to cook until the tomatoes are reduced to a paste-like consistency and the oil separates from the paste. Reduce the heat towards the end of the cooking time.

4 Add the meat, fenugreek leaves and water. Bring to the boil, reduce the heat to low, cover and simmer for 45–50 minutes, or until the meat is tender.

5 Heat a small saucepan over a low heat, then add the ghee. Stir in the garam masala. Cook for 30 seconds, then fold this spiced mixture into the curry. Remove from the heat, garnish with coriander sprigs and serve immediately with rice.

Meatballs in Creamy
Cashew Nut Sauce

Serves 4

ingredients

- 125 g/4½ oz cashew nuts
- 150 ml/5 fl oz boiling water
- 450 g/1 lb fresh lean minced lamb
- 1 tbsp thick set natural yogurt
- 1 medium egg, beaten
- ½ tsp ground cardamom
- ½ tsp ground nutmeg
- ½ tsp pepper
- ½ tsp dried mint
- ½ tsp salt, or to taste
- 300 ml/10 fl oz cold water
- 2.5-cm/1-inch piece cinnamon stick
- 5 green cardamom pods
- 5 cloves
- 2 bay leaves
- 3 tbsp sunflower oil or olive oil
- 1 onion, finely chopped
- 2 tsp garlic purée
- 1 tsp ground ginger
- 1 tsp ground fennel seeds
- ½ tsp ground turmeric
- ½–1 tsp chilli powder
- 150 ml/5 fl oz double cream
- 1 tbsp crushed pistachio nuts, to garnish
- naan bread, to serve

1 Place the cashew nuts in a small heatproof bowl with the boiling water and soak for 20 minutes.

2 Put the meat in a mixing bowl and add the yogurt, egg, ground cardamom, nutmeg, pepper, mint and salt. Knead until the mixture is smooth and velvety. Alternatively, put the ingredients in a food processor and process until fine. Chill the mixture for 30–40 minutes, then divide it into quarters. Make five balls out of each quarter and compress them so that they are firm, rolling them between your palms to make them smooth and neat.

3 Add the cold water to a large, shallow saucepan and bring to the boil, then add all the whole spices and the bay leaves. Arrange the meatballs in a single layer in the spiced liquid, reduce the heat to medium, cover the pan and cook for 12–15 minutes.

4 Remove the meatballs, cover and keep hot. Strain the spiced stock and set aside.

5 Wipe out the pan and add the oil. Place over a medium heat and add the onion and the garlic purée. Cook until the mixture begins to brown and add the ground ginger, ground fennel seeds, turmeric and chilli powder. Stir-fry for 2–3 minutes, then add the strained stock and meatballs. Bring to the boil, reduce the heat to low, cover and simmer for 10–12 minutes.

6 Meanwhile, purée the soaked cashew nuts in a blender and add to the meatball mixture along with the cream. Simmer for a further 5–6 minutes, then remove from the heat. Garnish with crushed pistachio nuts and serve immediately with naan bread.

Pork with Tamarind

Serves 6

ingredients

- 55 g/2 oz dried tamarind, roughly chopped
- 500 ml/18 fl oz boiling water
- 2 fresh green chillies, deseeded and roughly chopped
- 2 onions, roughly chopped
- 2 garlic cloves, roughly chopped
- 1 lemon grass stalk, bulb end roughly chopped
- 2 tbsp ghee or vegetable oil
- 1 tbsp ground coriander
- 1 tsp ground turmeric
- 1 tsp ground cardamom
- 1 tsp chilli powder
- 1 tsp ginger purée
- 1 cinnamon stick
- 1 kg/2 lb 4 oz diced pork fillet
- 1 tbsp chopped fresh coriander, plus extra sprigs to garnish
- sliced fresh red chillies, to garnish

1 Place the dried tamarind in a heatproof bowl, pour over the boiling water, mix well and leave to soak for 30 minutes.

2 Strain the soaking liquid through a sieve into a clean bowl, pressing down the pulp with the back of a wooden spoon. Discard the pulp. Pour 1 tablespoon of the tamarind liquid into a food processor and add the green chillies, onions, garlic and lemon grass and process until smooth.

3 Heat a large, heavy-based saucepan over a medium heat, then add the ghee. Add the chilli and onion paste, ground coriander, turmeric, cardamom, chilli powder, ginger purée and cinnamon stick and cook, stirring, for 2 minutes, or until the spices give off their aroma.

4 Add the pork and cook, stirring constantly, until lightly browned and well coated in the spice mixture. Pour in the remaining tamarind liquid, bring to the boil, then reduce the heat, cover and simmer for 30 minutes. Remove the lid from the pan and simmer for a further 30 minutes, or until the pork is tender. Stir in the chopped coriander and serve immediately, garnished with coriander sprigs and sliced red chillies.

Pork Vindaloo

Serves 4

ingredients

- 2–6 dried red chillies (long slim variety), torn into 2–3 pieces
- 5 cloves
- 2.5-cm/1-inch piece cinnamon stick, broken up
- 4 green cardamom pods
- ½ tsp black peppercorns
- ½ mace blade
- ¼ nutmeg, lightly crushed
- 1 tsp cumin seeds
- 1½ tsp coriander seeds
- ½ tsp fenugreek seeds
- 2 tsp garlic purée
- 1 tbsp ginger purée
- 3 tbsp cider vinegar or white wine vinegar
- 1 tbsp tamarind juice or juice of ½ lime
- 700 g/1 lb 9 oz boneless leg of pork, cut into 2.5-cm/1-inch cubes
- 6 tbsp sunflower oil
- 2 large onions, finely chopped
- 250 ml/9 fl oz lukewarm water, plus 4 tbsp
- 1 tsp salt, or to taste
- 1 tsp soft dark brown sugar
- 2 large garlic cloves, finely sliced
- 8–10 fresh or dried curry leaves
- cooked basmati rice and cooked okra, to serve

1 Grind the first 10 ingredients (all the spices) to a fine powder in a spice grinder. Transfer the ground spices to a bowl and add the garlic purée, ginger purée, vinegar and tamarind juice. Mix together to form a paste.

2 Put the pork in a large non-metallic bowl and rub about a quarter of the spice paste into the meat. Cover and leave to marinate in the refrigerator for 30–40 minutes.

3 Heat a medium-sized, heavy-based saucepan over a medium heat, then add 4 tablespoons of the oil. Add the onions and cook, stirring frequently, for 8–10 minutes until lightly browned. Add the remaining spice paste and cook, stirring constantly, for 5–6 minutes. Add 2 tablespoons of the water and cook until it has evaporated. Repeat with another 2 tablespoons of the water.

4 Add the marinated pork and cook over medium–high heat for 5–6 minutes until the meat changes colour. Add the salt, sugar and the remaining 250 ml/9 fl oz of the water. Bring to the boil, then reduce the heat to low, cover and leave to simmer for 50–55 minutes until the meat is tender.

5 Meanwhile, heat the remaining oil in a very small saucepan over a low heat. Add the sliced garlic and cook, stirring frequently, until it begins to brown. Add the curry leaves and leave to sizzle for 15–20 seconds. Stir the garlic mixture into the vindaloo. Remove from the heat and serve immediately with rice and okra.

Railway Pork & Vegetables

Serves 4–6

ingredients

- 40 g/1½ oz ghee or 3 tbsp vegetable oil or groundnut oil
- 1 large onion, finely chopped
- 4 green cardamom pods
- 3 cloves
- 1 cinnamon stick
- 1 tbsp Garlic and Ginger Paste (see page 15)
- 2 tsp garam masala
- ¼–½ tsp chilli powder
- ½ tsp ground asafoetida
- 2 tsp salt
- 600 g/1 lb 5 oz lean minced pork
- 1 potato, scrubbed and cut into 5-mm/¼-inch dice
- 400 g/14 oz canned chopped tomatoes
- 125 ml/4 fl oz water
- 1 bay leaf
- 1 large carrot, coarsely grated

1 Heat a flameproof casserole or large frying pan with a tight-fitting lid over a medium heat, then add the ghee. Add the onion and cook, stirring occasionally, for 5–8 minutes until golden brown. Add the cardamom pods, cloves and cinnamon stick and cook, stirring, for 1 minute, or until you can smell the aromas.

2 Add the garlic and ginger paste, garam masala, chilli powder, asafoetida and salt and stir for a further minute. Add the pork, using a wooden spoon to break up the meat, and cook for 5 minutes, or until no longer pink.

3 Add the potato, tomatoes, water and bay leaf and bring to the boil, stirring. Reduce the heat to the lowest level, cover tightly and simmer for 15 minutes. Stir in the carrot and simmer for a further 5 minutes, or until the potato and carrot are tender. Taste and adjust the seasoning, if necessary, and serve immediately.

Red Pork Curry
with Peppers

Serves 4

ingredients

- 2 tbsp vegetable oil or groundnut oil
- 1 onion, roughly chopped
- 2 garlic cloves, chopped
- 450 g/1 lb pork fillet, thickly sliced
- 1 red pepper, deseeded and cut into squares
- 175 g/6 oz mushrooms, quartered
- 2 tbsp Thai Red Curry Paste (see page 14)
- 115 g/4 oz creamed coconut, chopped
- 300 ml/10 fl oz pork stock or vegetable stock
- 2 tbsp Thai soy sauce
- 4 tomatoes, peeled, deseeded and chopped
- handful of fresh coriander, chopped, plus extra to garnish
- cooked rice noodles, to serve

1 Heat a wok over a medium–high heat, then add the oil. Add the onion and garlic and cook for 1–2 minutes until soft but not brown.

2 Add the pork slices and stir-fry for 2–3 minutes until brown all over. Add the red pepper, mushrooms and curry paste.

3 Dissolve the creamed coconut in the stock and add to the wok with the soy sauce. Bring to the boil and simmer for 4–5 minutes until the liquid has reduced and thickened.

4 Add the tomatoes and coriander and cook for 1–2 minutes. Garnish with extra chopped coriander and serve immediately with rice noodles.

Pork with Cinnamon & Fenugreek

Serves 4

ingredients

- 1 tsp ground coriander
- 1 tsp ground cumin
- 1 tsp chilli powder
- 1 tbsp dried fenugreek leaves
- 1 tsp ground fenugreek
- 150 ml/5 fl oz natural yogurt
- 450 g/1 lb diced pork fillet
- 4 tbsp ghee or vegetable oil
- 1 large onion, sliced
- 5-cm/2-inch piece fresh ginger, finely chopped
- 4 garlic cloves, finely chopped
- 1 cinnamon stick
- 6 green cardamom pods
- 6 whole cloves
- 2 bay leaves
- 175 ml/6 fl oz water
- salt

1 Mix the coriander, cumin, chilli powder, dried fenugreek, ground fenugreek and yogurt together in a small bowl. Place the pork in a large, shallow non-metallic dish and add the spice mixture, turning well to coat. Cover with clingfilm and leave to marinate in the refrigerator for 30 minutes.

2 Heat a large, heavy-based saucepan over a low heat, then add the ghee. Add the onion and cook, stirring occasionally, for 5 minutes, or until soft. Add the ginger, garlic, cinnamon stick, cardamom pods, cloves and bay leaves and cook, stirring constantly, for 2 minutes, or until the spices give off their aroma. Add the meat with its marinade and the water, and season to taste with salt. Bring to the boil, reduce the heat, cover and simmer for 30 minutes.

3 Meanwhile, heat a wok over a low heat, then transfer the meat mixture to the wok and cook, stirring constantly, until dry and tender. If necessary, occasionally sprinkle with a little water to prevent it sticking to the wok. Serve immediately.

Burmese Pork Curry

Serves 4

ingredients

- 700 g/1 lb 9 oz boned leg of pork, trimmed and cut into 2.5-cm/1-inch cubes
- 2 tbsp dry white wine
- 1 tsp salt, or to taste
- 8 large garlic cloves, roughly chopped
- 5-cm/2-inch piece fresh ginger, roughly chopped
- 2 fresh red chillies, roughly chopped
- 1 large onion, roughly chopped
- 1 tsp ground turmeric
- ½–1 tsp chilli powder
- 3 tbsp groundnut oil
- 1 tbsp sesame oil
- 200 ml/7 fl oz lukewarm water
- 1 fresh green chilli, deseeded and cut into julienne strips, to garnish
- cooked basmati rice, to serve

1 Mix the meat, wine and salt in a non-metallic bowl and set aside for 1 hour.

2 Put the garlic, ginger, chillies and onion in a food processor or blender and blend until the ingredients are mushy. Transfer to a bowl and stir in the turmeric and chilli powder.

3 Heat the groundnut oil and sesame oil in a medium-sized, heavy-based saucepan over a medium heat, then add the puréed ingredients. Stir and cook for 5–6 minutes, reduce the heat to low and continue to cook for a further 8–10 minutes, sprinkling over a tablespoon of water from time to time to prevent the spices sticking to the base of the pan.

4 Add the marinated pork, increase the heat to medium–high and stir until the meat changes colour. Pour in the water and bring to the boil. Reduce the heat to low, cover and cook for 1 hour 10 minutes, stirring several times during the last 15–20 minutes of the cooking time to prevent the thickened sauce sticking to the base of the pan. Remove from the heat and garnish with the strips of chilli. Serve immediately with rice.

Chapter 3
Fish & Seafood

Goan Fish Curry

Serves 4

ingredients

- 4 skinless salmon fillets, about 200 g/7 oz each
- 1 tsp salt, or to taste
- 1 tbsp lemon juice
- 3 tbsp sunflower oil
- 1 large onion, finely chopped
- 2 tsp garlic purée
- 2 tsp ginger purée
- ½ tsp ground turmeric
- 1 tsp ground coriander
- ½ tsp ground cumin
- ½–1 tsp chilli powder
- 250 ml/9 fl oz coconut milk
- 2–3 fresh green chillies, sliced lengthways
- 2 tbsp cider vinegar or white wine vinegar
- 2 tbsp chopped fresh coriander leaves
- cooked basmati rice, to serve

1 Cut each salmon fillet in half and lay on a plate in a single layer. Sprinkle with half the salt and all of the lemon juice and rub in gently. Cover and leave to marinate in the refrigerator for 15–20 minutes.

2 Heat a frying pan over a medium heat, then add the oil. Add the onion and cook, stirring frequently to ensure even colouring, for 8–9 minutes until a pale golden colour.

3 Add the garlic purée and ginger purée and cook, stirring, for 1 minute, then add the turmeric, ground coriander, cumin and chilli powder and cook, stirring, for 1 minute. Add the coconut milk, chillies and vinegar, then add the remaining salt, stir well and simmer, uncovered, for 6–8 minutes.

4 Add the fish and cook gently for 5–6 minutes. Stir in the fresh coriander and remove from the heat. Serve immediately with rice.

Cod Curry

Serves 4

ingredients

- 1 tbsp vegetable oil
- 1 small onion, chopped
- 2 garlic cloves, chopped
- 2.5-cm/1-inch piece fresh ginger, roughly chopped
- 2 large ripe tomatoes, peeled and roughly chopped
- 150 ml/5 fl oz fish stock
- 1 tbsp medium curry paste
- 1 tsp ground coriander
- 400 g/14 oz canned chickpeas, drained and rinsed
- 750 g/1 lb 10 oz cod fillet, cut into large chunks
- 4 tbsp chopped fresh coriander
- 4 tbsp natural yogurt
- salt and pepper
- cooked basmati rice, to serve

1 Heat a large saucepan over a low heat, then add the oil. Add the onion, garlic and ginger and cook for 4–5 minutes until soft. Remove from the heat. Put the onion mixture into a food processor or blender with the tomatoes and fish stock and process until smooth.

2 Add this mixture to the saucepan with the curry paste, ground coriander and chickpeas. Mix together well, then simmer gently for 15 minutes until thickened.

3 Add the pieces of fish and return to a simmer. Cook for 5 minutes until the fish is just tender. Remove from the heat and leave to stand for 2–3 minutes.

4 Stir in the coriander and yogurt. Season to taste with salt and pepper and serve immediately with rice.

Balti Fish Curry

Serves 4–6

ingredients

- 900 g/2 lb thick fish fillets, such as monkfish, grey mullet, cod or haddock, rinsed and cut into large chunks
- 2 bay leaves, torn
- 140 g/5 oz ghee or 150 ml/5 fl oz vegetable oil or groundnut oil
- 2 large onions, chopped
- ½ tbsp salt
- 150 ml/5 fl oz water
- chopped fresh coriander, to garnish
- naan bread, to serve

marinade

- ½ tbsp Garlic and Ginger Paste (see page 15)
- 1 fresh green chilli, deseeded and chopped
- 1 tsp ground coriander
- 1 tsp ground cumin
- ½ tsp ground turmeric
- ¼–½ tsp chilli powder
- 1 tbsp water
- salt

1 To make the marinade, mix the garlic and ginger paste, green chilli, ground coriander, cumin, turmeric and chilli powder together with salt to taste in a large bowl. Gradually stir in the water to form a thin paste. Add the fish chunks and smear with the marinade. Tuck the bay leaves underneath and leave to marinate in the refrigerator for at least 30 minutes, or up to 4 hours.

2 Remove the fish from the refrigerator 15 minutes in advance of cooking. Heat a wok over a medium–high heat, then add the ghee. Add the onions, sprinkle with the salt and cook, stirring frequently, for 8 minutes, or until very soft and golden.

3 Gently add the fish with its marinade and the bay leaves to the wok and stir in the water. Bring to the boil, then immediately reduce the heat and cook the fish for 4–5 minutes, spooning the sauce over the fish and carefully moving the chunks around, until they are cooked through and the flesh flakes easily. Adjust the seasoning, if necessary, then garnish with coriander and serve immediately with naan bread.

Malaysian Curry
with Red Snapper

Serves 6

ingredients

- 400 ml/14 fl oz canned coconut milk
- 3 tbsp desiccated coconut
- 2 tbsp groundnut oil
- 2 garlic cloves, finely chopped
- 2 spring onions, thinly sliced
- 2 fresh red chillies, deseeded and finely chopped
- 1 lemon grass stalk, finely chopped
- 2.5-cm/1-inch piece fresh ginger, thinly sliced
- 1 tbsp fish sauce
- 600 ml/1 pint fish or chicken stock
- 1 tbsp sugar
- ¾ tsp ground turmeric
- 2 tbsp lime juice
- 700 g/1 lb 9 oz red snapper fillets, thickly sliced
- salt
- lime wedges, to garnish

1 Pour the coconut milk into a strainer set over a bowl. Heat a wok over a medium–low heat, then add the desiccated coconut and dry-fry, stirring frequently, for 1–2 minutes until lightly browned. Add the oil, garlic, spring onions, chillies, lemon grass and ginger and stir-fry for 3 minutes.

2 Pour the thin coconut milk from the bowl into the wok, reserving the thick coconut milk in the strainer. Stir in the fish sauce, stock, sugar, turmeric and lime juice and season with salt. Bring just to the boil, then reduce the heat and simmer for 10 minutes.

3 Add the pieces of fish and simmer for a further 8–10 minutes until tender. Stir in the reserved coconut milk and simmer for a further 2–3 minutes until thickened. Serve immediately, garnished with lime wedges.

Thai Green Fish Curry

Serves 4

ingredients

- 2 tbsp vegetable oil
- 1 garlic clove, chopped
- 2 tbsp Thai Green Curry Paste
  (see page 14)
- 1 small aubergine, diced
- 125 ml/4 fl oz coconut milk
- 2 tbsp fish sauce
- 1 tsp sugar
- 225 g/8 oz firm white fish fillets,
  cut into pieces
- 125 ml/4 fl oz fish stock
- 2 kaffir lime leaves,
  finely shredded
- about 15 fresh Thai basil leaves
- fresh dill sprigs, to garnish

1 Heat a wok over a medium heat, then add the oil and heat until almost smoking. Add the garlic and cook until golden. Add the curry paste and stir-fry for a few seconds before adding the aubergine. Stir-fry for about 4–5 minutes until soft.

2 Add the coconut milk, bring to the boil and stir until it thickens and curdles slightly. Add the fish sauce and sugar to the wok and stir well.

3 Add the fish pieces and stock. Simmer for 3–4 minutes, stirring occasionally, until the fish is just tender. Add the lime leaves and basil, then cook for a further minute. Transfer to a warmed serving dish, then garnish with dill sprigs and serve immediately.

Rice Noodles with
Fried Yellow Fish

Serves 6

ingredients

- 450 g/1 lb fresh bun, or
  225 g/8 oz dried rice vermicelli,
  soaked in water until pliable
- 70 g/2½ oz rice flour or plain flour
- ½ tsp ground turmeric
- 900 g/2 lb white fish fillets,
  such as tilapia or flounder,
  cut into 2-cm/¾-inch cubes
- vegetable oil, for deep-frying,
  plus 2 tbsp for stir-frying
- 4 spring onions, trimmed and cut
  into 2.5-cm/1-inch lengths
- 24 fresh Thai basil leaves
- 24 sprigs fresh dill, trimmed
- 24 sprigs fresh coriander
- salt and pepper
- 50 g/1¾ oz dry-roasted unsalted
  peanuts, to garnish

1 If the bun has been refrigerated, reheat in boiling water for 2 seconds. Distribute the bun between six individual bowls. If using vermicelli, bring a medium-sized saucepan of water to the boil over a high heat. Put a handful of vermicelli in a sieve. Lower the sieve into the water and cook the vermicelli for 3–5 seconds, or until soft but still firm to the bite. Lift the sieve out and transfer the vermicelli to a large soup bowl. Repeat five more times for a total of six servings.

2 Put the flour and turmeric in a sealable polythene bag and season to taste with salt and pepper. Shake to mix well. Add the fish cubes, then seal the bag and shake to coat each fish cube evenly.

3 Heat a wok over a medium–high heat, then add the oil for deep-frying and heat to 180–190°C/350–375°F, or until a cube of bread browns in 30 seconds. Working in small batches, take a handful of fish cubes and shake off the excess flour, then lower into the hot oil. Deep-fry for 2–3 minutes, or until golden and crisp. Drain on a plate lined with kitchen paper.

4 Distribute the fried fish cubes evenly between each noodle serving.

5 Heat a separate wok over a high heat, then add the remaining 2 tablespoons of oil. Add the spring onions and stir-fry for 1 minute, or until fragrant and wilted. Add the basil, dill and coriander and stir-fry for 1–2 minutes, or until just wilted. Distribute the stir-fry evenly between the six bowls, garnish with peanuts and serve immediately.

Fish Korma

Serves 4

ingredients

- 700 g/1 lb 9 oz tilapia fillets, cut into 5-cm/2-inch pieces
- 1 tbsp lemon juice
- 1 tsp salt
- 55 g/2 oz cashew nuts
- 3 tbsp sunflower oil
- 5-cm/2-inch piece cinnamon stick, halved
- 4 green cardamom pods, bruised
- 2 cloves
- 1 large onion, finely chopped
- 1–2 fresh green chillies, chopped
- 2 tsp ginger purée
- 2 tsp garlic purée
- 150 ml/5 fl oz single cream
- 55 g/2 oz natural yogurt
- ¼ tsp ground turmeric
- ½ tsp sugar
- 1 tbsp toasted flaked almonds, to garnish
- naan bread, to serve

1 Place the fish on a large plate and gently rub in the lemon juice and ½ teaspoon of the salt. Set aside for 20 minutes. Place the cashew nuts in a heatproof bowl, pour over boiling water and soak for 15 minutes.

2 Heat a wide shallow saucepan over a low heat, then add the oil. Add the cinnamon, cardamom pods and cloves and leave them to sizzle for 30–40 seconds.

3 Add the onion, chillies, ginger purée and garlic purée. Increase the heat slightly and cook, stirring frequently, for 9–10 minutes until the onion is very soft.

4 Meanwhile, drain the cashew nuts and purée them with the cream and yogurt.

5 Stir the turmeric into the onion mixture and add the puréed ingredients, the remaining salt and the sugar. Mix thoroughly and arrange the fish in the sauce in a single layer. Bring to a slow simmer, cover the pan and cook for 5 minutes. Remove the lid and shake the pan gently from side to side. Spoon some of the sauce over the pieces of fish. Re-cover and cook for a further 3–4 minutes. Transfer to a serving dish and garnish with the toasted almonds. Serve immediately with naan bread.

Fish in Tomato & Chilli
Sauce with Fried Onion

Serves 4

ingredients

- 700 g/1 lb 9 oz tilapia fillets,
  cut into 5-cm/2-inch pieces
- 2 tbsp lemon juice
- 1 tsp salt, or to taste
- 1 tsp ground turmeric
- 4 tbsp sunflower oil
  plus extra for shallow-frying
- 2 tsp granulated sugar
- 1 large onion, finely chopped
- 2 tsp ginger purée
- 2 tsp garlic purée
- ½ tsp ground fennel seeds
- 1 tsp ground coriander
- ½–1 tsp chilli powder
- 175 g/6 oz canned chopped
  tomatoes
- 300 ml/10 fl oz lukewarm water
- 2–3 tbsp chopped fresh coriander
  leaves
- cooked basmati rice and
  poppadoms, to serve

1 Place the fish on a large plate and gently rub in the lemon juice, ½ teaspoon of the salt and ½ teaspoon of the turmeric. Set aside for 15–20 minutes.

2 Add enough oil for shallow-frying to cover the base of a 23-cm/9-inch frying pan to a depth of about 1 cm/½ inch and place over a medium–high heat. When the oil is hot, fry the pieces of fish, in a single layer, until well browned on both sides and a light crust is formed. Drain on kitchen paper.

3 Heat the 4 tablespoons of oil in a medium-sized saucepan or frying pan over a medium heat, then add the sugar. Allow it to brown, watching it carefully because once it browns it will blacken quickly. As soon as the sugar is brown, add the onion and cook for 5 minutes until soft. Add the ginger purée and garlic purée and cook for a further 3–4 minutes, or until the mixture begins to brown.

4 Add the ground fennel seeds, ground coriander, chilli powder and the remaining turmeric. Cook for about a minute, then add half the tomatoes. Stir and cook until the tomato juice has evaporated, then add the remaining tomatoes. Continue to cook, stirring, until the oil separates from the spice paste.

5 Pour in the water and add the remaining salt. Bring to the boil and reduce the heat to medium. Add the fish, stir gently, and reduce the heat to low. Cook, uncovered, for 5–6 minutes, then stir in half the chopped coriander and remove from the heat. Serve immediately, garnished with the remaining coriander and accompanied by rice and poppadoms.

Fish in Spicy Coconut Broth

Serves 6

ingredients

- 450 g/1 lb tilapia fillets
- 700 ml/1¼ pints hot water
- 1 lemon grass stalk
- 5-cm/2-inch piece fresh ginger
- 5–6 shallots or 1 large onion, roughly chopped
- 2 fresh red chillies, roughly chopped
- 4 large garlic cloves, roughly chopped
- 4 tbsp groundnut oil
- 1 tsp ground turmeric
- 1 tsp shrimp paste
- 1 tbsp fish sauce
- 500 g/1 lb 2 oz canned bamboo shoots in water
- 400 ml/14 fl oz coconut milk
- salt

to serve

- 200 g/7 oz rice noodles, cooked according to the instructions on the packet
- 4 hard-boiled eggs
- 8 dried red chillies, fried in a little oil until slightly blackened
- 4 spring onions (white part only), chopped
- lime or lemon wedges (optional)
- fish cakes or fritters

1 Put the fish in a large saucepan and pour in the hot water. Slice half the lemon grass and half the ginger and add to the fish. Bring to the boil, reduce the heat to low and simmer for 5–6 minutes. Switch off the heat, cover the pan and leave the ginger and lemon grass to infuse in the stock for 15–20 minutes.

2 Meanwhile, roughly chop the remaining lemon grass and ginger, put in a food processor or blender with the shallots, red chillies and garlic and blend until mushy.

3 Heat a large saucepan over a medium heat, then add the oil. Add the shallot mixture and turmeric and cook, stirring regularly, for 10–12 minutes, reducing the heat for the last few minutes of cooking. Sprinkle over a little water, if necessary, to prevent the mixture sticking.

4 Strain the fish stock, reserving the fish, and add enough water to make it up to 700 ml/1¼ pints. Pour into the pan along with the shrimp paste and fish sauce. Leave over a low heat while you prepare the bamboo shoots. Drain the bamboo shoots and chop into bite-sized pieces, then add to the pan with the coconut milk. Add salt to taste; both the shrimp paste and the fish sauce are salty so do make sure to taste before adding salt.

5 Break up the tilapia fillets into small pieces and add to the pan. Simmer, uncovered, for 5–6 minutes.

6 To serve, place the noodles in a bowl and top it up with the broth. Serve all the other accompaniments separately so that everyone can help themselves.

Penang Fish Curry

Serves 4

ingredients

- 25 g/1 oz dry-roasted peanuts
- 8–10 shallots or 2 onions, roughly chopped
- 2–3 fresh red chillies, roughly chopped
- 2.5-cm/1-inch piece fresh ginger, roughly chopped
- 4 large garlic cloves, roughly chopped
- 1 tsp shrimp paste
- 4 tbsp groundnut oil
- 1 tsp ground turmeric
- ½ tsp chilli powder
- 425 ml/15 fl oz lukewarm water
- ½ tsp salt, or to taste
- 2 tbsp tamarind juice
- ½ tsp sugar
- 700 g/1 lb 9 oz trout fillets, cut into 1-cm/½-inch slices
- fresh coriander sprigs, to garnish
- cooked basmati rice, to serve

1 Put the peanuts, shallots, chillies, ginger, garlic and shrimp paste in a food processor or blender and blend until the mixture is mushy. Remove and set aside.

2 Heat a large, shallow saucepan, preferably non-stick, over a medium heat, then add the oil. Add the peanut mixture, turmeric and chilli powder. Cook, stirring regularly, until the mixture begins to brown, then continue to cook until the mixture is fragrant, adding a little water from time to time to prevent it sticking to the base of the pan. This process will take 10–12 minutes.

3 Pour in the water and add the salt, tamarind juice and sugar. Stir and mix well and carefully add the fish. Stir gently to ensure that the fish is covered with the sauce. Cover the pan, reduce the heat to low and cook for 8–10 minutes. Remove from the heat and serve immediately, garnished with coriander sprigs and accompanied by rice.

Mixed Seafood Curry

Serves 4

ingredients

- 1 tbsp vegetable oil or
  groundnut oil
- 3 shallots, finely chopped
- 2.5-cm/1-inch piece fresh
  galangal, peeled and thinly sliced
- 2 garlic cloves, finely chopped
- 400 ml/14 fl oz coconut milk
- 2 lemon grass stalks,
  snapped in half
- 4 tbsp fish sauce
- 2 tbsp chilli sauce
- 225 g/8 oz raw tiger prawns,
  peeled and deveined
- 225 g/8 oz baby squid,
  cleaned and thickly sliced
- 225 g/8 oz salmon fillet,
  skinned and cut into chunks
- 175 g/6 oz tuna steak,
  cut into chunks
- 225 g/8 oz fresh mussels,
  scrubbed and debearded
- lime wedges, to garnish
- cooked jasmine rice, to serve

1 Heat a wok over a medium–high heat, then add the oil. Add the shallots, galangal and garlic and stir-fry for about 2 minutes until they start to soften. Add the coconut milk, lemon grass, fish sauce and chilli sauce. Bring to the boil, reduce the heat and simmer for 1–2 minutes.

2 Add the prawns, squid, salmon and tuna and simmer for 3–4 minutes until the prawns have turned pink and the fish is cooked.

3 Discard any mussels with broken shells or any that refuse to close when tapped with a knife. Add the remaining mussels to the wok and cover with a lid. Simmer for 1–2 minutes until they have opened. Discard any mussels that remain closed. Garnish with lime wedges and serve immediately with rice.

Goan-style Seafood Curry

Serves 4–6

ingredients

- 3 tbsp vegetable oil or groundnut oil
- 1 tbsp black mustard seeds
- 12 fresh curry leaves or 1 tbsp dried curry leaves
- 6 shallots, finely chopped
- 1 garlic clove, crushed
- 1 tsp ground turmeric
- ½ tsp ground coriander
- ¼–½ tsp chilli powder
- 140 g/5 oz creamed coconut, grated and dissolved in 300 ml/10 fl oz boiling water
- 500 g/1 lb 2 oz skinless, boneless white fish, such as monkfish or cod, cut into large chunks
- 450 g/1 lb large raw prawns, peeled and deveined
- finely grated rind and juice of 1 lime
- salt

1 Heat a wok over a high heat, then add the oil. Add the mustard seeds and stir for about 1 minute, or until they pop. Stir in the curry leaves.

2 Add the shallots and garlic and stir for about 5 minutes, or until the shallots are golden. Stir in the turmeric, coriander and chilli powder and continue stirring for about 30 seconds.

3 Add the dissolved creamed coconut. Bring to the boil, then reduce the heat to medium and stir for about 2 minutes.

4 Reduce the heat to low, add the fish and simmer for 1 minute, spooning the sauce over the fish and stirring it very gently. Add the prawns and continue to simmer for a further 4–5 minutes until the fish flakes easily and the prawns turn pink and curl.

5 Add half the lime juice, then taste and add more lime juice if necessary and salt to taste. Sprinkle with the lime rind and serve immediately.

Prawn Biryani

Serves 8

ingredients

- 1 tsp saffron strands
- 55 ml/2 fl oz lukewarm water
- 2 shallots, roughly chopped
- 3 garlic cloves, crushed
- 1 tsp chopped fresh ginger
- 2 tsp coriander seeds
- ½ tsp black peppercorns
- 2 cloves
- seeds from 2 green cardamom pods
- ½ cinnamon stick
- 1 tsp ground turmeric
- 1 fresh green chilli, chopped
- ½ tsp salt
- 2 tbsp ghee
- 1 tsp black mustard seeds
- 500 g/1 lb 2 oz raw tiger prawns, peeled and deveined
- 300 ml/10 fl oz coconut milk
- 300 ml/10 fl oz natural yogurt
- cooked basmati rice, to serve
- toasted flaked almonds and sliced spring onions, to garnish

1 Put the saffron in a small bowl with the water and soak for 10 minutes. Put the shallots, garlic, ginger, coriander seeds, peppercorns, cloves, cardamom pods, cinnamon stick, turmeric, chilli and salt into a spice grinder and grind to a paste.

2 Heat a saucepan over a high heat, then add the ghee. Add the mustard seeds and, when they start to pop, add the prawns and stir over a high heat for 1 minute. Stir in the spice mix, then the coconut milk and yogurt. Simmer for 20 minutes.

3 Spoon the prawn mixture into serving bowls. Top with the rice and drizzle over the saffron water. Serve immediately, garnished with the flaked almonds and spring onions.

Coconut Prawns with
Chillies & Curry Leaves

Serves 4

ingredients

- 4 tbsp sunflower oil
- ½ tsp black or brown mustard seeds
- ½ tsp fenugreek seeds
- 1 large onion, finely chopped
- 2 tsp garlic purée
- 2 tsp ginger purée
- 1–2 fresh green chillies, chopped
- 1 tbsp ground coriander
- ½ tsp ground turmeric
- ½ tsp chilli powder
- 1 tsp salt, or to taste
- 250 ml/9 fl oz coconut milk
- 450 g/1 lb cooked peeled tiger prawns, thawed if frozen
- 1 tbsp tamarind juice or juice of ½ lime
- ½ tsp crushed black peppercorns
- 10–12 fresh or dried curry leaves

1 Heat a wok over a medium–high heat, then add 3 tablespoons of the oil. When hot, but not smoking, add the mustard seeds, followed by the fenugreek seeds and the onion. Cook, stirring frequently, for 5–6 minutes until the onion is soft but not brown. Add the garlic purée, ginger purée and the chillies and cook, stirring frequently, for a further 5–6 minutes until the onion is a light golden colour.

2 Add the coriander, turmeric and chilli powder and cook, stirring, for 1 minute. Add the salt and coconut milk, followed by the prawns and tamarind juice. Bring to a slow simmer and cook, stirring occasionally, for 3–4 minutes.

3 Meanwhile, heat the remaining oil in a very small saucepan over a medium heat. Add the peppercorns and curry leaves. Turn off the heat and leave to sizzle for 20–25 seconds, then fold the aromatic oil into the prawn mixture. Remove from the heat and serve immediately.

Prawn Pooris

Serves 6

ingredients

- 2 tsp coriander seeds
- ½ tsp black peppercorns
- 1 large garlic clove, crushed
- 1 tsp ground turmeric
- ¼–½ tsp chilli powder
- ½ tsp salt
- 40 g/1½ oz ghee or 3 tbsp vegetable oil or groundnut oil
- 1 onion, grated
- 800 g/1 lb 12 oz canned crushed tomatoes
- pinch of sugar
- 500 g/1 lb 2 oz small cooked peeled prawns, thawed if frozen
- ½ tsp garam masala, plus extra to garnish
- 6 Pooris, kept warm (see page 200)
- fresh chopped coriander, to garnish

1 Put the coriander seeds, peppercorns, garlic, turmeric, chilli powder and salt in a spice grinder and blend to a thick paste.

2 Heat a wok over a low–medium heat, then add the ghee. Add the paste and cook, stirring constantly, for about 30 seconds.

3 Add the onion and stir for a further 30 seconds. Stir in the tomatoes and the sugar. Bring to the boil, stirring, and leave to bubble for 10 minutes or until reduced, mashing the tomatoes against the side of the wok to break them down. Taste and add extra salt, if necessary.

4 Add the prawns and sprinkle with the garam masala. When the prawns are hot, arrange the hot pooris on plates and top each one with a portion of the prawns. Sprinkle with the coriander and garam masala and serve immediately.

Tandoori Prawns

Serves 4

ingredients

- 4 tbsp natural yogurt
- 2 fresh green chillies, deseeded and chopped
- ½ tbsp Garlic and Ginger Paste (see page 15)
- seeds from 4 green cardamom pods
- 2 tsp ground cumin
- 1 tsp tomato purée
- ¼ tsp ground turmeric
- ¼ tsp salt
- pinch of chilli powder, ideally Kashmiri chilli powder
- 24 raw tiger prawns, thawed if frozen, peeled, deveined and tails left intact
- oil, for greasing
- lemon or lime wedges, to serve

1 Put the yogurt, chillies and garlic and ginger paste in a spice grinder and blend until a paste forms. Transfer the paste to a large non-metallic bowl and stir in the cardamom pods, cumin, tomato purée, turmeric, salt and chilli powder.

2 Add the prawns to the bowl and, using your hands, coat them with the yogurt marinade. Cover the bowl with clingfilm and chill for at least 30 minutes, or up to 4 hours.

3 When you are ready to cook, heat a large griddle or frying pan over a high heat until a few drops of water 'dance' when they hit the surface. Use crumpled kitchen paper or a pastry brush to grease the hot pan very lightly with oil.

4 Use tongs to lift the prawns out of the marinade, allowing the excess to drip back into the bowl, then place the prawns on the griddle and cook for 2 minutes. Flip them over and cook for a further 1–2 minutes until they turn pink, curl and are opaque all the way through (cut one to test). Serve immediately with lemon or lime wedges for squeezing over.

Chilli Prawns with
Garlic Noodles

Serves 4

ingredients

- 200 g/7 oz cooked peeled king or tiger prawns
- 4 tbsp sweet chilli sauce
- 2 tbsp groundnut oil or vegetable oil
- 4 spring onions, chopped
- 55 g/2 oz mangetout, trimmed and halved diagonally
- 1 tbsp Thai Red Curry Paste (see page 14)
- 400 ml/14 fl oz coconut milk
- 55 g/2 oz canned, drained bamboo shoots
- 55 g/2 oz fresh beansprouts

garlic noodles

- 115 g/4 oz dried medium egg noodles
- 2 tbsp groundnut oil or vegetable oil
- 2 garlic cloves, crushed
- handful of fresh coriander, chopped

1 Toss the prawns with the chilli sauce in a bowl. Cover and set aside.

2 Heat a wok over a medium–high heat, then add the oil. Add the spring onions and mangetout and stir-fry for 2–3 minutes. Add the curry paste and stir well. Pour in the coconut milk and bring gently to the boil, stirring occasionally. Add the bamboo shoots and beansprouts and cook, stirring, for 1 minute. Stir in the prawns and chilli sauce, reduce the heat and simmer for 1–2 minutes until just heated through.

3 Meanwhile, for the garlic noodles, cook the noodles according to the packet instructions. Drain and return to the pan.

4 Heat a small non-stick frying pan over high heat, then add the oil. Add the garlic and stir-fry over a high heat for 30 seconds. Add to the drained noodles with the coriander and toss together until well mixed.

5 Transfer the garlic noodles to serving bowls, top with the prawn mixture and serve immediately.

Goan Prawn Curry with
Hard-boiled Eggs

Serves 4

ingredients

- 4 tbsp sunflower oil
- 1 large onion, finely chopped
- 2 tsp ginger purée
- 2 tsp garlic purée
- 2 tsp ground coriander
- ½ tsp ground fennel
- ½ tsp ground turmeric
- ½–1 tsp chilli powder
- ½ tsp pepper
- 2–3 tbsp water
- 125 g/4½ oz canned chopped tomatoes
- 200 ml/7 fl oz coconut milk
- 1 tsp salt, or to taste
- 4 hard-boiled eggs
- 700 g/1 lb 9 oz cooked peeled tiger prawns
- juice of 1 lime
- 2–3 tbsp chopped fresh coriander leaves, plus extra sprigs to garnish
- cooked basmati rice, to serve

1 Heat a medium-sized saucepan over a medium–high heat, then add the oil. Add the onion and cook until soft but not brown. Add the ginger purée and garlic purée and cook for 2–3 minutes.

2 In a small bowl, mix the ground coriander, ground fennel, turmeric, chilli powder and pepper. Add the water and make a paste. Reduce the heat to medium, add this paste to the onion mixture and cook for 1–2 minutes. Reduce the heat to low and continue to cook for 3–4 minutes.

3 Add half the tomatoes to the pan and cook for 2–3 minutes, then add the remaining tomatoes and cook for a further 2–3 minutes.

4 Add the coconut milk and salt, bring to a slow simmer and cook, uncovered, for 6–8 minutes, stirring regularly.

5 Meanwhile, shell the eggs and, using a sharp knife, make four slits lengthways in each egg without cutting them through. Add the eggs to the pan along with the prawns. Increase the heat slightly and cook for 6–8 minutes.

6 Stir in the lime juice and chopped coriander. Remove from the heat and transfer the curry to a serving dish. Garnish with coriander sprigs and serve immediately with rice.

Mussels in Coconut Sauce

Serves 4

ingredients

- 1 kg/2 lb 4 oz live mussels, scrubbed and debearded
- 3 tbsp ghee or vegetable oil
- 1 onion, finely chopped
- 1 tsp garlic purée
- 1 tsp ginger purée
- 1 tsp ground cumin
- 1 tsp ground coriander
- ½ tsp ground turmeric
- pinch of salt
- 600 ml/1 pint canned coconut milk
- chopped fresh coriander, to garnish

1 Discard any mussels with broken shells and any that refuse to close when tapped with a knife.

2 Heat a large, heavy-based frying pan over a low heat, then add the ghee. Add the onion and cook, stirring occasionally, for 10 minutes, or until golden.

3 Add the garlic purée and ginger purée and cook, stirring constantly, for 2 minutes. Add the cumin, ground coriander, turmeric and salt and cook, stirring constantly, for a further 2 minutes. Stir in the coconut milk and bring to the boil.

4 Add the mussels, cover and cook for 5 minutes, or until the mussels have opened. Discard any mussels that remain closed. Transfer the mussels, with the coconut sauce, to a large warmed serving dish. Sprinkle with chopped coriander and serve immediately.

Mussels with Mustard
Seeds & Shallots

Serves 4

ingredients

- 2 kg/4 lb 8 oz live mussels, scrubbed and debearded
- 3 tbsp vegetable oil or groundnut oil
- ½ tbsp black mustard seeds
- 8 shallots, chopped
- 2 garlic cloves, crushed
- 2 tbsp distilled vinegar
- 4 small fresh red chillies
- 85 g/3 oz creamed coconut, dissolved in 300 ml/10 fl oz boiling water
- 10 fresh or 1 tbsp dried curry leaves
- ½ tsp ground turmeric
- ¼–½ tsp chilli powder
- salt

1 Discard any mussels with broken shells or any that refuse to close when tapped with a knife. Set aside.

2 Heat a wok over a medium–high heat, then add the oil. Add the mustard seeds and stir for about 1 minute, or until they start to pop.

3 Add the shallots and garlic and cook, stirring frequently, for 3 minutes, or until they start to brown. Stir in the vinegar, chillies, creamed coconut, curry leaves, turmeric, chilli powder and a pinch of salt and bring to the boil, stirring.

4 Reduce the heat to very low. Add the mussels, cover the wok and leave the mussels to simmer, shaking the wok frequently, for 3–4 minutes, or until they open. Discard any that remain closed. Ladle the mussels into deep bowls, then taste the broth and add extra salt, if necessary. Spoon the broth over the mussels and serve immediately.

Chapter 4
Vegetables & Pulses

Vegetable Korma

Serves 4

ingredients

- 85 g/3 oz cashew nuts
- 175 ml/6 fl oz boiling water
- good pinch of saffron threads, pounded
- 2 tbsp hot milk
- 1 small cauliflower, divided into 1-cm/½-inch florets
- 115 g/4 oz French beans, cut into 2.5-cm/1-inch lengths
- 115 g/4 oz carrots, cut into 2.5-cm/1-inch sticks
- 250 g/9 oz new potatoes, boiled in their skins and cooled
- 4 tbsp sunflower oil
- 1 large onion, finely chopped
- 2 tsp ginger purée
- 1–2 fresh green chillies, chopped
- 2 tsp ground coriander
- ½ tsp ground turmeric
- 6 tbsp lukewarm water
- 400 ml/14 fl oz good-quality vegetable stock
- ½ tsp salt, or to taste
- 2 tbsp single cream
- 2 tsp ghee or butter
- 1 tsp garam masala
- ¼ tsp grated nutmeg
- poppadoms, to serve

1 Place the cashew nuts in a heatproof bowl with the boiling water and soak for 20 minutes. Meanwhile place the saffron in a small bowl with milk and leave to soak.

2 Bring a saucepan of lightly salted water to the boil and blanch the vegetables, separately (the cauliflower will need 3 minutes, the beans 3 minutes, and the carrots 4 minutes), then drain and plunge in cold water. Peel the potatoes, if you like, and halve or quarter them according to their size.

3 Heat a medium-sized, heavy-based saucepan over a medium heat, then add the oil. Add the onion, ginger purée and chillies and cook, stirring frequently, for 5–6 minutes until the onion is soft. Add the coriander and turmeric and cook, stirring, for a further minute. Add 3 tablespoons of the water and cook for 2–3 minutes. Add the remaining water, then cook, stirring frequently, for 2–3 minutes, or until the oil separates from the spice paste.

4 Add the stock, saffron and milk mixture and salt, and bring to the boil. Drain the vegetables, add to the saucepan and return to the boil. Reduce the heat to low and simmer for 2–3 minutes. Meanwhile, put the cashew nuts and their soaking water in a food processor and process until well blended. Add to the korma, then stir in the cream. Leave to cook over a very low heat while you prepare the final seasoning.

5 Heat a very small saucepan over a low heat, then add the ghee. Add the garam masala and nutmeg and leave the spices to sizzle gently for 20–25 seconds. Fold the spiced butter into the korma. Remove from the heat and serve immediately, accompanied by poppadoms.

Vietnamese Vegetable Curry

Serves 6

ingredients

- 2 lemon grass stalks
- 50 ml/2 fl oz vegetable oil
- 3 large garlic cloves, crushed
- 1 large shallot, thinly sliced
- 2 tbsp Indian curry powder
- 700 ml/1¼ pints coconut milk
- 500 ml/18 fl oz coconut water
  (not coconut milk) or vegetable
  stock
- 2 tbsp fish sauce
- 4 fresh red bird's eye chillies
  or dried red Chinese (tien sien)
  chillies
- 6 kaffir lime leaves
- 1 carrot, peeled and cut
  diagonally into 1 cm/½ inch
  thick pieces
- 1 small–medium Asian aubergine,
  cut into 2.5-cm/1-inch pieces
- 1 small–medium bamboo shoot,
  cut into thin wedges
- 115 g/4 oz mangetout, topped
  and tailed
- 12 large shiitake mushrooms,
  stems discarded, caps halved
- 450 g/1 lb firm or extra-firm
  tofu, drained and cut into
  2.5-cm/1-inch cubes
- fresh chopped coriander and fried
  shallots, to garnish

1 Discard the bruised leaves and root ends of the lemon grass stalks, then cut 15–20 cm/6–8 inches of the lower stalks into paper-thin slices.

2 Heat a wok over a high heat, then add the oil. Add the garlic and shallot and stir-fry for 5 minutes, or until golden. Add the lemon grass and curry powder and stir-fry for 2 minutes, or until fragrant.

3 Add the coconut milk, coconut water, fish sauce, chillies and lime leaves and bring to the boil. Reduce the heat to low, then add the carrot and aubergine, cover and cook for 10 minutes.

4 Add the bamboo shoot, mangetout, mushrooms and tofu and cook for a further 5 minutes.

5 Serve immediately, garnished with the coriander and fried shallots.

Vegetables in a Creamy Tomato Sauce

Serves 4

ingredients

- 200 g/7 oz cauliflower, divided into 1-cm/½-inch florets
- 200 g/7 oz French beans, cut into 5-cm/2-inch lengths
- 200 g/7 oz baby carrots, peeled and left whole
- 200 g/7 oz boiled potatoes
- 4 tbsp sunflower oil
- 5 green cardamom pods, bruised
- 2 bay leaves
- 1 large onion, finely chopped
- 2.5-cm/1-inch piece fresh ginger, finely grated
- 1 tsp ground coriander
- ½ tsp ground cumin
- 1 tsp ground turmeric
- ½–1 tsp chilli powder
- 1 tbsp tomato purée
- 1 tsp salt, or to taste
- 150 ml/5 fl oz lukewarm water
- 150 ml/5 fl oz double cream
- 2 tomatoes, deseeded and roughly chopped
- naan bread, to serve

1 Bring a saucepan of lightly salted water to the boil and blanch the vegetables, separately (the cauliflower will need 3 minutes, the beans 3 minutes, and the carrots 4 minutes), then drain and plunge in cold water. Cut the potatoes into 2.5-cm/1-inch cubes.

2 Heat a medium-sized saucepan over a low heat, then add the oil. Add the cardamom pods and bay leaves. Allow them to sizzle for 30–40 seconds, then add the onion and ginger. Increase the heat to medium and cook for 5–6 minutes until the onion is soft, stirring regularly.

3 Add the coriander, cumin, turmeric and chilli powder. Cook for 2–3 minutes, then add a little water and continue to cook for a further minute. Add the tomato purée and cook for about a minute.

4 Drain the cauliflower, beans and carrots, and add to the pan along with the potatoes. Add the salt, stir and pour in the water. Cook, uncovered, for 2–3 minutes, then add the cream. Cook for 3–4 minutes, then fold in the tomatoes and remove from the heat. Serve immediately with some naan bread.

Vegetables with
Tofu & Spinach

Serves 4

ingredients

- vegetable oil or groundnut oil, for deep-frying, plus 2 tablespoons
- 225 g/8 oz firm tofu, drained and cut into cubes
- 2 onions, chopped
- 2 garlic cloves, chopped
- 1 fresh red chilli, deseeded and sliced
- 3 celery sticks, diagonally sliced
- 225 g/8 oz mushrooms, thickly sliced
- 115 g/4 oz baby corn cobs, cut in half
- 1 red pepper, deseeded and cut into strips
- 3 tbsp Thai Red Curry Paste (see page 14)
- 400 ml/14 fl oz coconut milk
- 1 tsp palm sugar or soft light brown sugar
- 2 tbsp Thai soy sauce
- 225 g/8 oz baby spinach leaves

1 Heat a wok over a high heat, then add the oil for deep-frying and heat to 180–190°C/350–375°F, or until a cube of bread browns in 30 seconds. Add the tofu, in batches, and cook for 4–5 minutes until crisp and brown all over. Remove with a slotted spoon and drain on kitchen paper.

2 Heat a separate wok over a medium heat, then add the 2 tablespoons of oil. Add the onions, garlic and chilli and stir-fry for 1–2 minutes until they start to soften. Add the celery, mushrooms, corn and red pepper and stir-fry for 3–4 minutes until they soften.

3 Stir in the curry paste and coconut milk and gradually bring to the boil. Add the sugar and soy sauce and then the spinach. Cook, stirring constantly, until the spinach has wilted. Serve immediately, topped with the tofu.

Cauliflower, Aubergine & Green Bean Korma

Serves 4–6

ingredients

- 85 g/3 oz cashew nuts
- 1½ tbsp Garlic and Ginger Paste (see page 15)
- 200 ml/7 fl oz water
- 55 g/2 oz ghee or 4 tbsp vegetable oil or groundnut oil
- 1 large onion, chopped
- 5 green cardamom pods, bruised
- 1 cinnamon stick, broken in half
- ¼ tsp ground turmeric
- 250 ml/9 fl oz double cream
- 140 g/5 oz new potatoes, scrubbed and chopped into 1-cm/½-inch pieces
- 140 g/5 oz cauliflower florets
- ½ tsp garam masala
- 140 g/5 oz aubergine, chopped into 2.5-cm/1-inch chunks
- 140 g/5 oz green beans, chopped into 2.5-cm/1-inch lengths
- salt and pepper
- chopped fresh mint or coriander, to garnish

1 Heat a large flameproof casserole or frying pan with a tight-fitting lid over a high heat. Add the cashew nuts and stir until they start to brown, then immediately tip them out of the casserole.

2 Put the nuts in a spice grinder with the garlic and ginger paste and 1 tablespoon of the water and whizz until a coarse paste forms.

3 Add the ghee to the casserole and melt over a medium–high heat. Add the onion and cook for 5–8 minutes until golden brown. Add the nut paste, stir for 5 minutes, then stir in the cardamom pods, cinnamon stick and turmeric.

4 Add the cream and the remaining water and bring to the boil, stirring. Reduce the heat to the lowest level, cover the casserole and simmer for 5 minutes.

5 Add the potatoes, cauliflower and garam masala and simmer, covered, for 5 minutes. Stir in the aubergine and green beans and continue simmering for a further 5 minutes, or until all the vegetables are tender. Check the sauce occasionally to make sure it isn't sticking to the base of the pan, and stir in a little water if needed.

6 Taste and add seasoning, if necessary. Sprinkle with the chopped mint and serve immediately.

Sweet & Sour Pumpkin

Serves 4–6

ingredients

- 1 kg/2 lb 4 oz pumpkin
- 4 tbsp sunflower oil
- 1 large onion, finely sliced
- 1–2 hot red chillies, deseeded and finely chopped
- 1 kg/2 lb 4 oz fresh ripe tomatoes, peeled and diced, or 800 g/1 lb 12 oz canned chopped tomatoes
- 1 tbsp sultanas
- 2 tbsp red wine vinegar
- finely grated rind and juice of 1 bitter orange or lemon

1 Peel, deseed and dice the pumpkin – you will need a very sharp knife.

2 Heat a wok over a very low heat, then add the oil. Add the onion and cook, stirring occasionally, for at least 15 minutes, or until soft and golden but not browned. Add the chillies and tomatoes and heat until bubbling. Reduce the heat and simmer for 20–30 minutes, or until all the ingredients reduce to a jammy sauce.

3 Stir in the pumpkin, sultanas, vinegar and orange rind and juice. cook until it bubbles up again, then reduce the heat and cook, loosely covered, for a further 20 minutes, or until the flavours are well blended and the pumpkin is perfectly tender. Serve at room temperature.

Vegetable Curry

Serves 6

ingredients

- 3 tbsp groundnut oil
- ½ tsp cumin seeds
- ½ tsp mustard seeds
- ½ tsp onion seeds
- 1 large onion, thinly sliced
- 3 curry leaves
- 1½ tsp grated fresh ginger
- 3 green chillies, deseeded and finely chopped
- 3 tbsp medium-hot curry paste
- 2 carrots, thickly sliced
- 175 g/6 oz French beans, cut into short lengths
- 1 cauliflower, broken into florets
- 3 tomatoes, peeled and diced
- pinch of chilli powder (optional)
- ½ tsp ground turmeric
- 85 g/3 oz frozen peas, thawed
- 225 ml/8 fl oz vegetable stock
- salt

1 Heat a saucepan over a low heat, then add the oil. Add the cumin, mustard and onion seeds and cook, stirring frequently, for 2 minutes until they begin to give off their aroma. Add the onion and curry leaves and cook, stirring occasionally, for 5 minutes until the onion has softened.

2 Add the ginger and chillies and cook, stirring frequently, for 2 minutes, then stir in the curry paste and cook for a further 5 minutes. Add the carrots, beans and cauliflower, mix well and cook, stirring occasionally, for a further 5 minutes.

3 Add the tomatoes, stir in the chilli powder, if using, and turmeric, season with salt and cook for 3–4 minutes. Add the peas and cook for a further 5 minutes.

4 Pour in the stock, cover and simmer, stirring occasionally, for 15 minutes, or until all the vegetables are tender. Taste and adjust the seasoning, if necessary, then serve immediately.

Okra Stir-fried with Onions

Serves 4

ingredients

- 280 g/10 oz okra
- 1 small red pepper
- 1 onion
- 2 tbsp sunflower oil
- 1 tsp black or brown mustard
  seeds
- ½ tsp cumin seeds
- 3 large garlic cloves,
  lightly crushed, then chopped
- ½ tsp chilli powder
- ½ tsp salt, or to taste
- ½ tsp garam masala
- cooked basmati rice, to serve

1 Scrub each okra gently, rinse well in cold running water, then slice off the hard head. Halve diagonally and set aside.

2 Remove the seeds and core from the red pepper and cut into 4-cm/1-inch strips. Halve the onion lengthways and cut into 5 mm/¼ inch thick slices.

3 Heat a wok over a medium heat, then add the oil. When hot but not smoking, add the mustard seeds, followed by the cumin seeds.

4 Remove from the heat and add the garlic. Return to a low heat and cook the garlic gently, stirring, for 1 minute, or until lightly browned.

5 Add the okra, red pepper and onion, increase the heat to medium–high and stir-fry for 2 minutes. Add the chilli powder and salt and stir-fry for a further 3 minutes. Add the garam masala and stir-fry for 1 minute. Remove from the heat and serve immediately with rice.

Red Curry with
Mixed Leaves

Serves 4

ingredients

- 2 tbsp groundnut oil or vegetable oil
- 2 onions, thinly sliced
- 1 bunch of fine asparagus spears
- 400 ml/14 fl oz coconut milk
- 2 tbsp Thai Red Curry Paste (see page 14)
- 3 fresh kaffir lime leaves
- 225 g/8 oz baby spinach leaves
- 2 heads pak choi, chopped
- 1 small head Chinese leaves, shredded
- handful of fresh coriander, chopped
- cooked jasmine rice, to serve

1 Heat a wok over a medium–high heat, then add the oil. Add the onions and asparagus and stir-fry for 1–2 minutes.

2 Add the coconut milk, curry paste and lime leaves and bring gently to the boil, stirring occasionally. Add the spinach, pak choi and Chinese leaves and cook, stirring, for 2–3 minutes until wilted. Add the coriander and stir well. Serve immediately with rice.

Cumin-scented
Aubergine & Potato Curry

Serves 4

ingredients

- 1 large aubergine, about 350 g/12 oz
- 225 g/8 oz potatoes, boiled in their skins and cooled
- 3 tbsp sunflower oil
- ½ tsp black mustard seeds
- ½ tsp nigella seeds
- ½ tsp fennel seeds
- 1 onion, finely chopped
- 2.5-cm/1-inch piece fresh ginger, grated
- 2 fresh green chillies, chopped
- ½ tsp ground cumin
- 1 tsp ground coriander
- 1 tsp ground turmeric
- ½ tsp chilli powder
- 1 tbsp tomato purée
- 450 ml/15 fl oz lukewarm water
- 1 tsp salt, or to taste
- ½ tsp garam masala
- 2 tbsp chopped fresh coriander leaves
- naan bread, to serve

1 Quarter the aubergine lengthways and cut the stem end of each quarter into 5-cm/2-inch pieces. Halve the remaining part of each quarter and cut into the same size as above. Soak the aubergine pieces in cold water.

2 Peel the potatoes and cut into 5-cm/2-inch cubes. Heat a large saucepan over a medium heat, then add the oil. When hot, add the mustard seeds and, as soon as they start popping, add the nigella seeds and fennel seeds.

3 Add the onion, ginger and chillies and cook for 7–8 minutes until the mixture begins to brown.

4 Add the cumin, ground coriander, turmeric and chilli powder. Cook for about a minute, then add the tomato purée. Cook for a further minute, pour in the water, then add the salt and aubergine. Bring to the boil and cook over a medium heat for 8–10 minutes, stirring frequently to ensure that the aubergine cooks evenly. At the start of cooking, the aubergine will float, but once it soaks up the liquid it will sink quickly. As soon as this happens, add the potatoes and cook for 2–3 minutes, stirring.

5 Stir in the garam masala and chopped coriander and remove from the heat. Serve immediately with naan bread.

Butternut Squash Curry

Serves 4

ingredients

- 2 tbsp groundnut oil or vegetable oil
- 1 tsp cumin seeds
- 2 red onions, sliced
- 2 celery sticks, sliced
- 1 large butternut squash, peeled, deseeded and cut into chunks
- 2 tbsp Thai Green Curry Paste (see page 14)
- 300 ml/10 fl oz vegetable stock
- 2 fresh kaffir lime leaves
- 55 g/2 oz fresh beansprouts
- handful of fresh coriander, chopped, to garnish
- cooked jasmine rice, to serve

1 Heat a wok over a medium–high heat, then add the oil. Add the cumin seeds and stir-fry for 2–3 minutes until they are starting to pop. Add the onions and celery and stir-fry for 2–3 minutes, then add the squash and stir-fry for 3–4 minutes. Add the curry paste, stock and lime leaves and bring to the boil, stirring occasionally.

2 Reduce the heat and simmer gently for 3–4 minutes until the squash is tender. Add the beansprouts and cook for a further 1–2 minutes until hot but still crunchy. Scatter the coriander over the curry and serve immediately with rice.

Courgette & Cashew
Nut Curry

Serves 4

ingredients

- 2 tbsp vegetable oil or groundnut oil
- 6 spring onions, chopped
- 2 garlic cloves, chopped
- 2 fresh green chillies, deseeded and chopped
- 450 g/1 lb courgettes, cut into thick slices
- 115 g/4 oz shiitake mushrooms, halved
- 55 g/2 oz beansprouts
- 85 g/3 oz cashew nuts, toasted or dry-fried
- a few Chinese chives, snipped
- 4 tbsp Thai soy sauce
- 1 tsp fish sauce
- cooked noodles, to serve

1 Heat a wok over a medium–high heat, then add the oil. Add the spring onions, garlic and chillies and cook for 1–2 minutes until soft but not brown.

2 Add the courgettes and mushrooms and cook for 2–3 minutes until tender.

3 Add the beansprouts, cashew nuts, chives, soy sauce and fish sauce and stir-fry for 1–2 minutes.

4 Serve hot with noodles.

Mushroom Bhaji

Serves 4

ingredients

- 280 g/10 oz closed-cup white mushrooms
- 4 tbsp sunflower oil
- 1 onion, finely chopped
- 1 fresh green chilli, finely chopped
- 2 tsp garlic purée
- 1 tsp ground cumin
- 1 tsp ground coriander
- ½ tsp chilli powder
- ½ tsp salt, or to taste
- 1 tbsp tomato purée
- 3 tbsp water
- 1 tbsp snipped fresh chives, to garnish

1 Wipe the mushrooms with damp kitchen paper and slice thickly.

2 Heat a medium-sized saucepan over a medium heat, then add the oil. Add the onion and chilli and cook, stirring frequently, for 5–6 minutes until the onion is soft but not brown. Add the garlic purée and cook, stirring, for 2 minutes.

3 Add the cumin, coriander and chilli powder and cook, stirring, for 1 minute. Add the mushrooms, salt and tomato purée and stir until all the ingredients are thoroughly blended.

4 Sprinkle the water evenly over the mushrooms and reduce the heat to low. Cover and cook for 10 minutes, stirring halfway through. The sauce should have thickened, but if it appears runny, cook, uncovered, for 3–4 minutes, or until you achieve the desired consistency.

5 Transfer to a serving dish, sprinkle with chives and serve immediately.

Spiced Black-eyed
Beans & Mushrooms

Serves 4

ingredients

- 1 onion, roughly chopped
- 4 large garlic cloves, roughly chopped
- 2.5-cm/1-inch piece fresh ginger, roughly chopped
- 4 tbsp sunflower oil
- 1 tsp ground cumin
- 1 tsp ground coriander
- ½ tsp ground fennel
- 1 tsp ground turmeric
- ½–1 tsp chilli powder
- 175 g/6 oz canned chopped tomatoes
- 400 g/14 oz canned black-eyed beans, drained and rinsed
- 115 g/4 oz large flat mushrooms, wiped and cut into bite-sized pieces
- ½ tsp salt, or to taste
- 175 ml/6 fl oz lukewarm water
- 1 tbsp chopped fresh mint
- 1 tbsp chopped fresh coriander leaves
- naan bread, to serve

1 Purée the onion, garlic and ginger in a food processor or blender.

2 Heat a medium-sized saucepan over a medium heat, then add the oil. Add the puréed ingredients and cook for 4–5 minutes, then add the cumin, ground coriander, ground fennel, turmeric and chilli powder. Stir-fry for about a minute, then add the tomatoes. Cook until the tomatoes are pulpy and the juice has evaporated.

3 Add the black-eyed beans, mushrooms and salt. Stir well and pour in the water, bring to the boil, cover the pan and reduce the heat to low. Simmer for 8–10 minutes, stirring halfway through.

4 Stir in the chopped mint and coriander and remove from the heat. Transfer to a serving dish and serve as a main course with naan bread or as an accompaniment to meat, fish or poultry dishes.

Garden Peas & Paneer in
Chilli-tomato Sauce

Serves 4

ingredients

- 4 tbsp sunflower oil
- 250 g/9 oz Paneer, cut into 2.5-cm/1-inch cubes (see page 16)
- 4 green cardamom pods, bruised
- 2 bay leaves
- 1 onion, finely chopped
- 2 tsp garlic purée
- 2 tsp ginger purée
- 2 tsp ground coriander
- ½ tsp ground turmeric
- ½–1 tsp chilli powder
- 150 g/5½ oz canned chopped tomatoes
- 425 ml/15 fl oz lukewarm water, plus 2 tbsp
- 1 tsp salt, or to taste
- 125 g/4½ oz frozen peas
- ½ tsp garam masala
- 2 tbsp single cream
- 2 tbsp chopped fresh coriander leaves
- naan bread, to serve

1 Heat a medium-sized, non-stick saucepan over a medium heat, then add 2 tablespoons of the oil. Add the paneer and cook, stirring frequently, for 3–4 minutes, or until evenly browned. Paneer tends to splatter in hot oil, so stand slightly away from the hob. Alternatively, use a splatter screen. Remove the paneer from the pan and drain on kitchen paper.

2 Add the remaining oil to the saucepan and reduce the heat to low. Add the cardamom pods and bay leaves and leave to sizzle gently for 20–25 seconds. Add the onion, increase the heat to medium and cook, stirring frequently, for 4–5 minutes until the onion is soft. Add the garlic purée and ginger purée and cook, stirring frequently, for a further 3–4 minutes until the onion is a pale golden colour.

3 Add the ground coriander, turmeric and chilli powder and cook, stirring, for 1 minute. Add the tomatoes and cook, stirring frequently, for 4–5 minutes. Add the 2 tablespoons of water and cook, stirring frequently, for 3 minutes, or until the oil separates from the spice paste.

4 Add the remaining water and the salt. Bring to the boil, then reduce the heat to low and simmer, uncovered, for 7–8 minutes.

5 Add the paneer and peas and simmer for 5 minutes. Stir in the garam masala, cream and chopped coriander and remove from the heat. Serve immediately with some naan bread.

Chickpeas in Coconut Milk

Serves 4

ingredients
- 275 g/9¾ oz potatoes, cut into 1-cm/½-inch cubes
- 250 ml/9 fl oz hot water
- 400 g/14 oz canned chickpeas, drained and rinsed
- 250 ml/9 fl oz coconut milk
- 1 tsp salt, or to taste
- 2 tbsp sunflower oil
- 4 large garlic cloves, finely chopped or crushed
- 2 tsp ground coriander
- ½ tsp ground turmeric
- ½–1 tsp chilli powder
- juice of ½ lemon
- cooked basmati rice, to serve

1 Put the potatoes in a medium-sized saucepan with the hot water. Bring to the boil, then reduce the heat to low and cook, covered, for 6–7 minutes. Add the chickpeas and cook, uncovered, for 3–4 minutes until the potatoes are tender.

2 Add the coconut milk and salt and bring to a slow simmer.

3 Meanwhile, heat a small saucepan over a low heat, then add the oil. Add the garlic and cook, stirring frequently, until it begins to brown. Add the coriander, turmeric and chilli powder and cook, stirring, for 25–30 seconds.

4 Fold the aromatic oil into the chickpeas. Stir in the lemon juice and remove from the heat. Serve hot with rice.

Lentils with Fresh Chillies,
Mint & Coriander

Serves 4

ingredients

- 85 g/3 oz red split lentils (masoor dhal)
- 85 g/3 oz skinless split chickpeas (channa dhal)
- 3 tbsp sunflower oil
- 1 onion, finely chopped
- 2–3 fresh green chillies, chopped
- 2 tsp garlic purée
- 2 tsp ginger purée
- 1 tsp ground cumin
- 600 ml/1 pint lukewarm water
- 1 tsp salt, or to taste
- 1 tbsp chopped fresh mint
- 1 tbsp chopped fresh coriander leaves
- 55 g/2 oz unsalted butter
- 1 fresh green chilli and 1 small tomato, deseeded and cut into julienne strips, to garnish

1 Wash the lentils and chickpeas together until the water runs clear and leave to soak for 30 minutes.

2 Heat a medium-sized saucepan, preferably non-stick, over a medium heat, then add the oil. Add the onion, chillies, garlic purée and ginger purée. Stir-fry the mixture until it begins to brown.

3 Drain the lentils and chickpeas and add to the onion mixture together with the cumin. Reduce the heat to low and stir-fry for 2–3 minutes, then pour in the water. Bring to the boil, reduce the heat to low, cover and simmer for 25–30 minutes.

4 Stir in the salt, mint, coriander and butter. Stir until the butter has melted, then remove from the heat. Serve hot, garnished with chilli and tomato strips.

Mixed Lentils with
Five-spice Seasoning

Serves 4

ingredients

- 125 g/4½ oz red split lentils (masoor dhal)
- 125 g/4½ oz skinless split mung beans (mung dhal)
- 900 ml/1½ pints hot water
- 1 tsp ground turmeric
- 1 tsp salt, or to taste
- 1 tbsp lemon juice
- 2 tbsp sunflower oil
- ¼ tsp black mustard seeds
- ¼ tsp cumin seeds
- ¼ tsp nigella seeds
- ¼ tsp fennel seeds
- 4–5 fenugreek seeds
- 2–3 dried red chillies
- 1 small tomato, deseeded and cut into strips, and fresh coriander sprigs, to garnish
- naan bread, to serve

1 Mix the lentils and beans together and wash until the water runs clear. Put them into a large saucepan with the hot water. Bring to the boil and reduce the heat slightly. Leave to boil for 5–6 minutes and, when the foam subsides, add the turmeric, reduce the heat to low, cover and cook for 20 minutes. Add the salt and lemon juice and beat the dhal with a wire whisk. Add a little more hot water if the dhal is too thick.

2 Heat a small saucepan over a medium heat, then add the oil. When hot, but not smoking, add the mustard seeds. As soon as they begin to pop, reduce the heat to low and add the cumin seeds, nigella seeds, fennel seeds, fenugreek seeds and chillies. Leave the spices to sizzle until the seeds begin to pop and the chillies have blackened. Pour the contents of the saucepan over the lentils, scraping every bit out of the saucepan.

3 Turn off the heat and keep the lentils covered until you are ready to serve. Transfer to a serving dish and garnish with tomato strips and coriander sprigs. Serve hot as a main course with naan bread or as an accompaniment to meat, fish or poultry dishes.

Lentils with Cumin & Shallots

Serves 4

ingredients

- 200 g/7 oz red split lentils (masoor dhal)
- 850 ml/1½ pints water
- 1 tsp salt, or to taste
- 2 tsp sunflower oil
- ½ tsp black or brown mustard seeds
- ½ tsp cumin seeds
- 4 shallots, finely chopped
- 2 fresh green chillies, chopped
- 1 tsp ground turmeric
- 1 tsp ground cumin
- 1 fresh tomato, chopped
- 2 tbsp chopped fresh coriander leaves

1 Wash the lentils until the water runs clear and put into a medium-sized saucepan. Add the water and bring to the boil. Reduce the heat to medium and skim off the foam. Cook, uncovered, for 10 minutes. Reduce the heat to low, cover and cook for 45 minutes, stirring occasionally to ensure that the lentils do not stick to the base of the pan as they thicken. Stir in the salt.

2 Meanwhile, heat a small saucepan over a medium heat, then add the oil. When hot, but not smoking, add the mustard seeds, followed by the cumin seeds. Add the shallots and chillies and cook, stirring, for 2–3 minutes, then add the turmeric and ground cumin. Add the tomato and cook, stirring, for 30 seconds.

3 Fold the shallot mixture into the cooked lentils. Stir in the coriander, remove from the heat and serve immediately.

Egg & Lentil Curry

Serves 4

ingredients

- 3 tbsp ghee or vegetable oil
- 1 large onion, chopped
- 2 garlic cloves, chopped
- 2.5-cm/1-inch piece fresh ginger, chopped
- ½ tsp minced chilli or chilli powder
- 1 tsp ground coriander
- 1 tsp ground cumin
- 1 tsp paprika
- 85 g/3 oz red split lentils (masoor dhal)
- 450 ml/16 fl oz vegetable stock
- 225 g/8 oz canned chopped tomatoes
- 6 eggs
- 55 ml/2 fl oz coconut milk
- 2 tomatoes, cut into wedges
- salt
- fresh coriander sprigs, to garnish
- chapattis, to serve

1 Heat a saucepan over a low heat, then add the ghee. Add the onion and cook gently for 3 minutes. Stir in the garlic, ginger, chilli and spices and cook gently, stirring frequently, for 1 minute. Stir in the lentils, stock and tomatoes and bring to the boil. Reduce the heat, cover and simmer, stirring occasionally, for 30 minutes until the lentils are tender.

2 Meanwhile, place the eggs in a saucepan of cold water and bring to the boil. Reduce the heat and simmer for 10 minutes. Drain and cover immediately with cold water.

3 Stir the coconut milk into the lentil mixture and season well with salt. Process the mixture in a blender or food processor until smooth. Return to the pan and heat through.

4 Shell the hard-boiled eggs and cut into quarters. Divide the hard-boiled egg quarters and tomato wedges between four serving plates. Spoon over the hot lentil sauce and garnish with coriander sprigs. Serve hot with chapattis.

Chapter 5
Sides & Accompaniments

Onion Bhajis

Serves 4

ingredients

- 150 g/5½ oz gram flour
- 1 tsp salt, or to taste
- small pinch of bicarbonate of soda
- 25 g/1 oz ground rice
- 1 tsp fennel seeds
- 1 tsp cumin seeds
- 2 green chillies, finely chopped
- 2 large onions, about 400 g/14 oz, sliced into half-rings and separated
- 15 g/½ oz fresh coriander, including the tender stalks, finely chopped
- 200 ml/7 fl oz water
- sunflower oil, for deep-frying
- Mango Chutney (see page 219) or tomato chutney, to serve

1 Sift the gram flour into a large bowl and add the salt, bicarbonate of soda, ground rice, fennel seeds and cumin seeds. Mix together thoroughly, then add the chillies, onions and coriander. Gradually pour in the water and mix until a thick batter has formed and all the other ingredients are thoroughly coated with it.

2 Heat a wok over a high heat, then add the oil and heat to 180–190°C/350–375°F, or until a cube of bread browns in 30 seconds. If the oil is not hot enough, the bhajis will be soggy. Add as many ½ tablespoons of the batter as will fit in a single layer, without overcrowding.

3 Reduce the heat slightly and cook the bhajis for 8–10 minutes until golden brown and crisp. Maintaining a steady temperature is important to ensure that the centres of the bhajis are cooked, while the outsides turn brown. Remove and drain on kitchen paper. Keep hot in a low oven while you cook the remaining batter. Serve hot with chutney.

Vegetarian Samosas

Makes 8

ingredients
- 1 carrot, diced
- 200 g/7 oz sweet potato, diced
- 85 g/3 oz frozen peas
- 2 tbsp ghee or vegetable oil
- 1 onion, chopped
- 1 garlic clove, chopped
- 2.5-cm/1-inch piece fresh ginger, grated
- 1 tsp ground turmeric
- 1 tsp ground cumin
- ½ tsp chilli powder
- ½ tsp garam masala
- 1 tsp lime juice
- vegetable oil, for frying
- salt and pepper
- lime wedges and Mango Chutney (see page 219), to serve

pastry
- 150 g/5½ oz plain flour, plus extra for dusting
- 3 tbsp butter, diced
- 4 tbsp warm milk

1 Bring a saucepan of water to the boil, add the carrot and cook for 4 minutes. Add the sweet potato and cook for 4 minutes, then add the peas and cook for a further 3 minutes. Drain.

2 Heat a saucepan over a medium heat, then add the ghee. Add the onion, garlic, ginger, spices and lime juice and cook, stirring, for 3 minutes. Add the vegetables and season to taste with salt and pepper. Cook, stirring, for 2 minutes. Remove from the heat and leave to cool for 15 minutes.

3 To make the pastry, put the flour into a bowl and rub in the butter. Add the milk and mix to form a dough. Knead briefly and divide into 4 pieces.

4 On a lightly floured work surface, roll into balls, then roll out into rounds 17 cm/6½ inches in diameter. Halve each round, divide the filling between them and brush the edges with water, then fold over into triangles and seal the edges.

5 Heat 2.5 cm/1 inch of oil in a frying pan to 180–190°C/350–375°F, or until a cube of bread browns in 30 seconds. Cook the samosas in batches for 3–4 minutes, or until golden. Drain on kitchen paper and serve hot with lime wedges and mango chutney.

Bombay Potatoes

Serves 6

ingredients

- 500 g/1 lb 2 oz new potatoes, diced
- 1 tsp ground turmeric
- pinch of salt
- 4 tbsp ghee or vegetable oil
- 6 curry leaves
- 1 dried red chilli
- 2 fresh green chillies, chopped
- ½ tsp nigella seeds
- 1 tsp mixed mustard and onion seeds
- ½ tsp cumin seeds
- ½ tsp fennel seeds
- ¼ tsp asafoetida
- 2 onions, chopped
- 5 tbsp chopped fresh coriander
- juice of ½ lime

1 Place the potatoes in a large, heavy-based saucepan and pour in just enough cold water to cover. Add ½ teaspoon of the turmeric and the salt and bring to the boil. Simmer for 10 minutes, or until tender, then drain and reserve until required.

2 Heat a large, heavy-based frying pan over a medium–high heat, then add the ghee. Add the curry leaves and dried red chilli and cook, stirring frequently, for a few minutes, or until the chilli is blackened. Add the remaining turmeric, the fresh chillies, the nigella seeds, mustard seeds, onion seeds, cumin seeds, fennel seeds, asafoetida, onions and coriander and cook, stirring constantly, for 5 minutes, or until the onions have softened.

3 Add the potatoes, stir and cook over a low heat, stirring frequently, for 10 minutes, or until the potatoes have heated through. Squeeze over the lime juice and serve immediately.

Chapattis

Makes 16

ingredients

- 400 g/14 oz chapatti flour (atta), plus extra for dusting
- 1 tsp salt
- ½ tsp granulated sugar
- 2 tbsp sunflower oil
- 250 ml/9 fl oz lukewarm water

1 Mix the flour, salt and sugar together in a large bowl. Add the oil and work well into the flour mixture with your fingertips. Gradually add the water, mixing at the same time. When the dough is formed, transfer to a work surface and knead for 4–5 minutes. The dough is ready when all the excess moisture has been absorbed by the flour. Alternatively, mix the dough in a food processor. Wrap the dough in clingfilm and leave to rest for 30 minutes.

2 Divide the dough in half, then cut each half into eight equal-sized pieces. Form each piece into a ball and flatten into a round cake. Dust each cake lightly in flour and roll out to a 15-cm/6-inch round. Keep the remaining cakes covered while you are working on one. The chapattis will cook better when freshly rolled out, so roll them out and cook them one at a time.

3 Heat a heavy-based cast-iron griddle or a large, heavy-based frying pan over a medium–high heat. Put a chapatti on the griddle and cook for 30 seconds. Using a fish slice, turn it over and cook until bubbles begin to appear on the surface. Turn it over again. Press the edges down gently with a clean cloth to encourage the chapatti to puff up – they will not always puff up, but this doesn't matter. Cook until brown patches appear on the underside. Remove from the pan and keep hot by wrapping in a piece of foil lined with kitchen paper. Repeat with the remaining chapattis. Serve warm.

Chilli-coriander Naan

Makes 8

ingredients

- 450 g/1 lb plain flour
- 2 tsp sugar
- 1 tsp salt
- 1 tsp baking powder
- 1 egg
- 250 ml/9 fl oz milk
- 2 tbsp sunflower oil, plus extra for oiling
- 2 fresh red chillies, chopped
- 15 g/½ oz fresh coriander leaves, chopped
- 2 tbsp butter, melted

1 Sift the flour, sugar, salt and baking powder together into a large bowl. Whisk the egg and milk together and gradually add to the flour mixture, mixing it with a wooden spoon, until a dough is formed.

2 Transfer the dough to a work surface, make a depression in the centre of the dough and add the oil. Knead for 3–4 minutes until the oil is absorbed by the flour and you have a smooth and pliable dough. Wrap the dough in clingfilm and leave to rest for 1 hour.

3 Divide the dough into eight equal-sized pieces, form each piece into a ball and flatten into a thick cake. Cover the dough cakes with clingfilm and leave to rest for 10–15 minutes.

4 Preheat the grill to high. Line a grill pan with a piece of foil and brush with oil.

5 The traditional shape of naan is teardrop, but you can make them any shape you wish. To make the traditional shape, roll each flattened cake into a 13-cm/5-inch round and pull the lower end gently. Carefully roll out again, maintaining the teardrop shape, to about 23 cm/9 inches across at the widest point. Alternatively, roll the flattened cakes out to 23-cm/9-inch rounds.

6 Mix the chillies and coriander together, then divide into eight equal portions and spread a portion on the surface of each naan. Press gently so that the mixture sticks to the dough.

7 Transfer a naan to the prepared grill pan and cook 13 cm/5 inches below the heat source for 1 minute, or until slightly puffed and brown patches appear on the surface. As soon as brown spots appear on the surface turn over and cook the other side for 45–50 seconds until lightly browned. Remove from the grill and brush with the melted butter. Wrap the cooked naans in a tea towel while you cook the remaining naans. Serve warm.

Pooris

Makes 12

ingredients

- 225 g/8 oz wholemeal flour, sifted, plus extra for dusting
- ½ tsp salt
- 25 g/1 oz ghee, melted
- 100–150 ml/3½–5 fl oz water
- vegetable oil or groundnut oil, for deep-frying

1 Put the flour and salt into a bowl and drizzle the ghee over the surface. Gradually stir in the water until a stiff dough forms.

2 Turn out the dough onto a lightly floured work surface and knead for 10 minutes, or until it is smooth and elastic. Shape the dough into a ball and place it in the cleaned bowl, then cover with a damp tea towel and leave to rest for 20 minutes.

3 Divide the dough into 12 equal-sized pieces and roll each into a ball. Working with one ball of dough at a time, flatten the dough between your palms, then thinly roll it out on a lightly floured work surface into a 13-cm/5-inch round. Continue until all the dough balls are rolled out.

4 Heat a wok over high heat, then add oil to a depth of at least 7.5 cm/3 inches and heat until it reaches 180–190°C/350–375°F, or until a cube of bread browns in 30 seconds. Drop one poori into the hot fat and fry for about 10 seconds, or until it puffs up. Use two large spoons to flip the poori over and spoon some hot oil over the top.

5 Use the two spoons to lift the poori from the oil and allow any excess oil to drip back into the wok. Drain the poori on crumpled kitchen paper and serve immediately. Continue until all the pooris are fried, making sure the oil returns to the correct temperature before you add another poori. Serve warm.

Dosas

Makes 8

ingredients

- 115 g/4 oz basmati rice, rinsed
- 70 g/2½ oz split black lentils (urad dal chilke)
- ¼ tsp fenugreek seeds
- 125 ml/4 fl oz water
- 25 g/1 oz ghee, melted
- salt

1 Bring a saucepan of lightly salted water to the boil, add the rice and boil for 5 minutes, then drain. Put the rice, lentils and fenugreek seeds in a bowl with water to cover and leave to soak overnight.

2 The next day, strain the rice and lentils, reserving the soaking liquid. Put the rice and lentils in a food processor with 75 ml/2½ fl oz of the water and whizz until a smooth, sludgy grey paste forms. Slowly add the remaining water.

3 Cover the bowl with a tea towel that has been soaked in hot water and wrung out and leave to ferment in a warm place for 5–6 hours, until small bubbles appear all over the surface.

4 Stir the mixture and add as much extra water as necessary to get a consistency of single cream. Add salt to taste. The amount of salt you need depends on how sour-tasting the batter is.

5 Heat a large frying pan over a high heat until a splash of water 'dances' when it hits the surface, then brush the surface with melted ghee. Put a ladleful of batter in the centre of the pan and use the base of the ladle to spread it out as thinly as possible, then leave it to cook for 2 minutes until it is golden brown and crisp on the base.

6 Flip the dosa over and continue cooking for a further 2 minutes. Turn it out of the pan and keep warm if you are going to wrap it around a filling, or leave to cool. Continue until all the batter has been used.

Spiced Basmati Rice

Serves 4

ingredients
- 225 g/8 oz basmati rice
- 25 g/1 oz ghee or 2 tbsp vegetable oil or groundnut oil
- 5 green cardamom pods, bruised
- 5 cloves
- 2 bay leaves
- ½ cinnamon stick
- 1 tsp fennel seeds
- ½ tsp black mustard seeds
- 450 ml/16 fl oz water
- 1½ tsp salt, or to taste
- 2 tbsp chopped fresh coriander
- pepper

1 Rinse the rice in several changes of water until the water runs clear, then leave to soak for 30 minutes. Drain and set aside until ready to cook.

2 Heat a casserole or large saucepan with a tight-fitting lid over a medium–high heat, then add the ghee. Add the spices and stir for 30 seconds. Stir the rice into the casserole so the grains are coated with ghee. Stir in the water and salt and bring to the boil.

3 Reduce the heat to as low as possible and cover the casserole tightly. Simmer, without lifting the lid, for 8–10 minutes, until the grains are tender and all the liquid has been absorbed.

4 Turn off the heat and use two forks to mix in the coriander. Adjust the seasoning to taste. Re-cover the pan and leave to stand for 5 minutes before serving.

Mint & Coriander Rice with
Toasted Pine Kernels

Serves 4

ingredients

- good pinch of saffron threads, pounded
- 2 tbsp hot milk
- 225 g/8 oz basmati rice
- 2 tbsp sunflower oil
- 5-cm/2-inch piece cinnamon stick, broken in half
- 4 green cardamom pods, bruised
- 2 star anise
- 2 bay leaves
- 450 ml/16 fl oz lukewarm water
- 3 tbsp chopped fresh coriander
- 2 tbsp chopped fresh mint
- 1 tsp salt, or to taste
- 25 g/1 oz pine kernels

1 Put the saffron threads in a small bowl with the milk and set aside until you are ready to use it.

2 Wash the rice in several changes of cold water until the water runs clear. Leave to soak in fresh cold water for 20 minutes, then leave to drain in a colander.

3 Heat a medium-sized, heavy-based saucepan over a low heat, then add the oil. Add the cinnamon, cardamom pods, star anise and bay leaves and leave to sizzle gently for 20–25 seconds. Add the rice and stir well to ensure that the grains are coated with the flavoured oil.

4 Add the water, stir once and bring to the boil. Add the saffron and milk, coriander, mint and salt and boil for 2–3 minutes. Cover tightly, reduce the heat to very low and cook for 7–8 minutes. Turn off the heat and leave to stand, covered, for 7–8 minutes.

5 Meanwhile, preheat a small heavy-based frying pan over a medium heat, add the pine kernels and cook, stirring, until they begin to glisten with their natural oils and are lightly toasted. Transfer to a plate and leave to cool.

6 Add half the pine kernels to the rice and fluff up the rice with a fork. Transfer to a serving dish, garnish with the remaining pine kernels and serve immediately.

Lemon-laced Basmati Rice

Serves 4

ingredients
- 225 g/8 oz basmati rice
- 2 tbsp sunflower oil
- ½ tsp black or brown mustard seeds
- 10–12 curry leaves, preferably fresh
- 25 g/1 oz cashew nuts
- ¼ tsp ground turmeric
- 1 tsp salt, or to taste
- 450 ml/16 fl oz hot water
- 2 tbsp lemon juice

1 Wash the rice in several changes of cold water until the water runs clear. Leave to soak in fresh cold water for 20 minutes, then leave to drain in a colander.

2 Heat a non-stick saucepan over a medium heat, then add the oil. When hot, but not smoking, add the mustard seeds, followed by the curry leaves and the cashew nuts.

3 Stir in the turmeric, quickly followed by the rice and salt. Cook, stirring, for 1 minute, then add the hot water and lemon juice. Stir once, bring to the boil and boil for 2 minutes. Cover tightly, reduce the heat to very low and cook for 8 minutes. Turn off the heat and leave to stand, covered, for 6–7 minutes. Fork through the rice and transfer to a serving dish. Serve immediately.

Pilau Rice

Serves 2–4

ingredients

- 200 g/7 oz basmati rice
- 2 tbsp ghee
- 3 green cardamom pods
- 2 whole cloves
- 3 black peppercorns
- ½ tsp salt
- ½ tsp saffron threads
- 400 ml/14 fl oz water

1 Rinse the rice in several changes of water until the water runs clear, then leave to soak for 30 minutes. Drain and set aside until ready to cook.

2 Heat a heavy-based saucepan over a medium–high heat, then add the ghee. Add the cardamom pods, cloves and peppercorns and stir-fry for 1 minute. Add the rice and stir-fry for a further 2 minutes.

3 Add the salt, saffron and water to the rice mixture and reduce the heat. Cover the saucepan and leave to simmer over a low heat for 20 minutes until all the water has evaporated.

4 Transfer the rice to a large, warmed serving dish and serve hot.

Cucumber Raita

Serves 4–5

ingredients
- 1 small cucumber
- 175 g/6 oz natural yogurt
- ¼ tsp granulated sugar
- ¼ tsp salt
- 1 tsp cumin seeds
- 10–12 black peppercorns
- ¼ tsp paprika

1 Peel the cucumber and scoop out the seeds. Cut the flesh into bite-sized pieces and set aside.

2 Put the yogurt into a bowl and beat with a fork until smooth. Add the sugar and salt and mix well.

3 Heat a small, heavy-based saucepan over a medium–high heat. When the pan is hot, turn off the heat and add the cumin seeds and peppercorns. Stir for 40–50 seconds, until they release their aroma.

4 Remove from the pan and leave to cool for 5 minutes, then crush in a mortar with a pestle or on a hard surface with a rolling pin.

5 Reserve ¼ teaspoon of this mixture and stir the remainder into the yogurt. Add the cucumber and stir to mix. Transfer the raita to a serving dish and sprinkle with the reserved toasted spices and the paprika.

Chilli & Onion Chutney

Makes 225 g/8 oz

ingredients

- 1–2 fresh green chillies, finely chopped
- 1 small fresh bird's eye chilli, finely chopped
- 1 tbsp white wine vinegar or cider vinegar
- 2 onions, finely chopped
- 2 tbsp fresh lemon juice
- 1 tbsp sugar
- 3 tbsp chopped fresh coriander, mint or parsley, or a combination of herbs
- salt
- chilli flower, to garnish

1 Put the chillies in a small non-metallic bowl with the vinegar, stir and then drain. Return the chillies to the bowl and stir in the onions, lemon juice, sugar and herbs, then add salt to taste.

2 Leave to stand at room temperature or cover and chill for 15 minutes. Garnish with the chilli flower before serving.

Coconut Sambal

Makes 140 g/5 oz

ingredients

- 125 g/4½ oz desiccated coconut
- 2 fresh green chillies, chopped
- 2.5-cm/1-inch piece fresh ginger, peeled and finely chopped
- 4 tbsp chopped fresh coriander
- 2 tbsp lemon juice, or to taste
- 2 shallots, very finely chopped

1 Put the coconut and chillies in a food processor and process for about 30 seconds, until finely chopped. Add the ginger, coriander and lemon juice and process again.

2 If the mixture seems too dry, stir in about 1 tablespoon of water. Stir in the shallots and serve immediately, or cover and chill until required.

Mango Chutney

Makes 250 g/9 oz

ingredients

- 1 large mango, about 400 g/ 14 oz, peeled, stoned and finely chopped
- 2 tbsp lime juice
- 1 tbsp vegetable oil or groundnut oil
- 2 shallots, finely chopped
- 1 garlic clove, finely chopped
- 2 fresh green chillies, deseeded and finely sliced
- 1 tsp black mustard seeds
- 1 tsp coriander seeds
- 5 tbsp palm sugar or soft light brown sugar
- 5 tbsp white wine vinegar
- 1 tsp salt
- pinch of ground ginger

1 Put the mango in a non-metallic bowl with the lime juice and set aside.

2 Heat a large frying pan or saucepan over a medium–high heat, then add the oil. Add the shallots and cook for 3 minutes. Add the garlic and chillies and stir for a further 2 minutes, or until the shallots are soft but not brown. Add the mustard seeds and coriander seeds and stir.

3 Add the mango to the pan with the sugar, vinegar, salt and ginger and stir. Reduce the heat to its lowest setting and simmer for 10 minutes until the liquid thickens and the mango becomes sticky.

4 Remove from the heat and leave to cool completely. Transfer to an airtight container, then cover and chill for 3 days before using.

Conversion Charts

temperatures

CELSIUS (°C)	GAS	FAHRENHEIT (°F)
110	¼	225
120	½	250
140	1	275
150	2	300
160	3	325
180	4	350
190	5	375
200	6	400
220	7	425
230	8	450
240	9	475

weight measures

METRIC	IMPERIAL
5 G	⅛ OZ
10 G	¼ OZ
15 G	½ OZ
25/30 G	1 OZ
35 G	1¼ OZ
40 G	1½ OZ
50 G	1¾ OZ
55 G	2 OZ
60 G	2¼ OZ
70 G	2½ OZ
85 G	3 OZ
90 G	3¼ OZ
100 G	3½ OZ
115 G	4 OZ
125 G	4½ OZ
140 G	5 OZ
150 G	5½ OZ
175 G	6 OZ
200 G	7 OZ
225 G	8 OZ
250 G	9 OZ
275 G	9¾ OZ
280 G	10 OZ
300 G	10½ OZ
325 G	11½ OZ
350 G	12 OZ
375 G	13 OZ
400 G	14 OZ
425 G	15 OZ
450 G	1 LB
500 G	1 LB 2 OZ

volume measures

METRIC	IMPERIAL
1.25 ML	¼ TSP
2.5 ML	½ TSP
5 ML	1 TSP
10 ML	2 TSP
15 ML	1 TBSP/3 TSP
30 ML	2 TBSP
45 ML	3 TBSP
60 ML	4 TBSP
75 ML	5 TBSP
90 ML	6 TBSP
15 ML	½ FL OZ
30 ML	1 FL OZ
50 ML	2 FL OZ
75 ML	2½ FL OZ
100 ML	3½ FL OZ
125 ML	4 FL OZ
150 ML	5 FL OZ
175 ML	6 FL OZ
200 ML	7 FL OZ
225 ML	8 FL OZ
250 ML	9 FL OZ
300 ML	10 FL OZ
350 ML	12 FL OZ
400 ML	14 FL OZ
425 ML	15 FL OZ
450 ML	16 FL OZ
500 ML	18 FL OZ
600 ML	1 PINT